THE CHURCH COMES FROM ALL NATIONS

Concordia Academic Press

SEMINARY EDITORIAL COMMITTEE
Charles Arand, Concordia Seminary, St. Louis, Missouri
Charles Gieschen, Concordia Theological Seminary, Ft. Wayne, Indiana
Paul Raabe, Concordia Seminary, St. Louis, Missouri
Peter Scaer, Concordia Theological Seminary, Ft. Wayne, Indiana
Detlev Schulz, Concordia Theological Seminary, Ft. Wayne, Indiana
James Voelz, Concordia Seminary, St. Louis, Missouri

THE CHURCH COMES FROM ALL NATIONS

LUTHER TEXTS ON MISSION

VOLKER STOLLE

TRANSLATED BY
KLAUS DETLEV SCHULZ AND DANIEL THIES

CONCORDIA PUBLISHING HOUSE • SAINT LOUIS
ACADEMIC PRESS

English translation copyright © 2003 Concordia Publishing House
Published by Concordia Academic Press, a division of Concordia Publishing House
3558 S. Jefferson Ave., St. Louis, MO 63118-3968

All rights reserved. No part of this publication may be reproduced, stored in a retrieval system, or transmitted, in any form or by any means, electronic, mechanical, photocopying, recording, or otherwise, without the prior written permission of Concordia Publishing House.

Originally published as *Kirche aus allen Völkern: Luther-Texte zur Mission* by Verlag der Ev.-Luth.~Mission, Erlangen (now Erlanger Verlag für Mission und Ökumene), © 1983.

Quotations from vols. 2, 6, 7, 14, 20, 24 of Luther's Works, American Edition, copyright © 1960, 1970, 1965, 1958, 1973, 1961, used by permission of Concordia Publishing House.

Quotations from vols. 39, 43, 45, 46, 53 of Luther's Works, American Edition, edited by Eric W. Gritsch, Gustav K. Wiencke, Walther I. Brandt, Robert C. Schultz, and Ulrich S. Leupold respectively, copyright © 1970, 1968, 1962, 1967, 1965, used by permission of Augsburg Publishing House.

Scripture quotations marked (NIV) are taken from the Holy Bible, New International Version®. NIV®. Copyright © 1973, 1978, 1984 by International Bible Society. Used by permission of Zondervan Publishing House. All rights reserved.

Manufactured in the United States of America

Library of Congress Cataloging-in-Publication Data

Luther, Martin, 1483-1546.
 [Kirche aus allen Vèolkern. English]
 The church comes from all nations : Luther texts on mission / [compiled by] Volker Stolle ; translated by Klaus Detlev Schulz and Daniel Thies.
    p. cm.
 Includes bibliographical references (p.   ).
 ISBN 0-7586-0546-3
 1. Lutheran Church--Doctrines. 2. Missions—Theory. I. Stolle, Volker. II. Title.
BX8065.3.L8813 2003
266'.41—dc21

2003011448

1 2 3 4 5 6 7 8 9 10   12 11 10 09 08 07 06 05 04 03

Contents

Translators' Foreword	9
Preface	11
I. Biblical Foundation for Mission	13

All Christians from the patriarchs to us ourselves are called to mission

Steadfastness in faith leads toward a missionary expansion of faith	15
Abraham was effective as a missionary in Egypt	16
Jacob preaches to the Gentiles	17
Mary and Joseph were missionaries in Egypt like the Wise Men were in their land. Persecution leads to the expansion of the church.	18
On the missionary effectiveness of the treasurer in Africa	19
A Christian lives for the sake of proclamation	20
Every Christian is bound by duty to give a missionary witness	21
The missionary witness is linked to prayer	23

The movement that began with the apostles continues until Judgment Day

As a stone that falls in the water	24
The kingdom of Christ is a constant happening	26
We are still calling today	27

The preaching of Christ is God's blessing for all people—as preaching of Law and Gospel

The whole of theology is therein summarized	28
The preaching of repentance and forgiveness of sins addresses all people	30
Reformation of mission practice	34

II. Practical Realization of Mission — 41

Congregational work with missionary orientation
- Missionary forms of liturgy — 43
- Catechetical instruction as preparation for missionary witness — 46
- The singing of Christian songs as Gospel witness — 47
- Hymns — 48

Mission prayers
- Your kingdom come — 51
- Lord, convert — 52

The missionary witness toward the Jews
- Biblical teaching and Christian life must come together — 53
- Common hearing of the witness of the Bible — 56
- The missionary conversation must not demand too much of our Jewish partners — 60
- Luther reports on his conversations with Jews — 61
- The meaning of the Reformation for the Jewish mission — 62
- Instructions on the Baptism of a Jewish maiden — 63
- Conversion or banishment — 65

The missionary witness toward the Turks
- The missionary responsibility of the pastoral office — 66
- How righteous Christians should confront the Turks — 67
- It is chiefly a spiritual confrontation — 68
- The Qur'an is to be tested by the witness to Christ — 70
- Prisoners of war as missionaries — 71

III. The History of Mission — 75

The mission stretches through all time from the beginning to the end of the world
- From the beginning of the world, Christ has been preached and believed — 77
- The different religions must be derived from the one true religion — 79
- Only the preaching of Christ actually makes God known — 80

The movement of the Gospel through the world before the coming of the end	82
The end of the preaching of the Gospel is near	84

The church of God must resist the church of Satan

Mission and reformation are very closely connected. This is already demonstrated by the biblical example of Egypt.	85
The church always lives in severe tribulation	87
The last confrontation between church and antichurch	89

The worldwide gathering of the people of God

How Christianity spread through the world	91
The gathering of a people of God from all peoples	96
Now there are still many islands and lands that have been newly discovered	98
God fulfills his promise in the history of mission	100

Epilogue 103
Biblical References 107
Selected Bibliography 111

Translators' Foreword

Translation is most effectively done in a team. Difficulties are smoothed out easier and mistakes detected far quicker. I am thus indebted to Pastor Daniel Thies who, as a student in my course "Theology of Missions," offered to translate the major portion of the original text—*Kirche aus allen Völkern: Luther-Texte zur Mission ausgewählt und zusammengestellt von Volker Stolle*—which had been published in 1983 by the Verlag der Ev.-Luth. Mission Erlangen (now named "Erlanger Verlag für Mission und Ökumene").

With the publication of this translation, we hope to fill a noticeable gap in Anglo-Saxon Lutheran missiology. The author, Volker Stolle, professor of New Testament and Missiology at Oberursel and former mission director of the Lutheran Church Mission (formerly Bleckmar mission), has enthusiastically embraced our endeavor and seized this occasion to forward to us a number of additional sources. This translated version, therefore, is more expansive than its German original.

We also acknowledge the publishers Augsburg Fortress and Concordia with whose permission we made use of Luther's Works, American Edition (cited as LW). Translations of biblical texts were already provided therein. In other instances, they are either our own or taken from the New International Version. Additional citations are made to the Weimar Edition (WA, WATr, WABr).

Klaus Detlev Schulz
Associate Professor
Chairman Pastoral Ministry and Missions
Concordia Theological Seminary, Ft. Wayne, Indiana

Daniel Thies,
Pastor, Eternal Trinity Church, Milton, Florida

Preface

It was thought for a long time that Luther had little to say concerning questions of missions. A century that established missionary undertakings with worldwide goals as pioneering achievements was disappointed not to find with Luther a comparable organized mission practice. After all, the discovery of America and the sea passage to India at the end of the fifteenth century had opened up a wider view of the world. Luther appeared, because of his internal struggle and a certain landlocked provincial attitude, to have overlooked the great world missionary challenges.

Meanwhile, the picture has changed. The activist missionary understanding of the previous generations has itself fallen into a crisis. New developments to some extent have overtaken it. New problems have received emphasis. Mission is no longer understood as a thing that plays itself out chiefly on the outer edges of Christendom but as a way of life or, rather, as a lifestyle for every Christian congregation within its particular surrounding. Here, Luther now begins to speak with surprising wisdom. He has expressed insights on the topic of missions that are, to a certain degree, of exciting relevance. One notices the close relationship between the concern of the Reformation and of missions. One is made conscious of the connection of life and doctrine in missionary witness. Luther becomes meaningful for various questions concerning the missionary task of the Christian and the church.

This collection of texts organizes several excerpts according to thematic criteria. In so doing, a strict systematic order is not maintained.

Rather, certain considerations recur in different aspects, and connected remarks occasionally are separated and placed in different contexts. The excerpts have been carefully adapted to fit the modern language to eliminate as much as possible difficulties in understanding. Latin texts are given in German translation.

Bergen-Bleckmar, February 18, 1983
Volker Stolle

I

BIBLICAL FOUNDATION FOR MISSION

Luther lives and thinks with the Bible. Holy Scripture is a book that has transferred its message from the close quarters of the people of Israel into the wider ethnic world. It is a missionary book. This could not but have an influence on Luther because of his intensive study of this Scripture. Consequently, Luther takes the missionary witness of every Christian so much for granted that he himself attests to it even where the text itself does not address it. Nearness to Scripture also means for Luther that the missionary expansion, which occurred in biblical times, is neither past nor complete. Instead, it is a living, contemporary, and personal reality of life. From the impact of the biblical message of Law and Gospel on his own person, Luther, who lived outside the biblical geography, professes unequivocally that if it is meant for him, then also all people without exception are in need of this preaching and should hear it. The foreign nature and peculiarity of God's Word exclude both the combination of missionary proclamation with human goals of imperialism and cultural export, as well as confessional rivalry.

All Christians from the Patriarchs to Us Ourselves Are Called to Mission

Steadfastness in faith leads toward a missionary expansion of faith

Genesis 12:8b (*author's translation*): And Abram built an altar to the Lord and called out [not upon] the name of the Lord.

Here you should note the godliness of the holy patriarch. Even though the people who lived at Moreh were beginning to hate him chiefly on account of his religion, yet this does not cause Abraham to give up his devotion to his religion. On the contrary, he erects an altar on this mountain, which is midway between Bethel and Ai, in order to perform his duty as bishop; that is, he instructs his church concerning the will of God, admonishes them to lead a holy life, strengthens them in their faith, fortifies their hope of future blessing, and prays with them. The Hebrew verb includes all these things. I have preferred to leave the words as they appear in the Hebrew text and not to follow our translator, who explains them as dealing merely with calling upon God.[44]

Lectures on Genesis (LW 2:286)
Genesis-Vorlesung 1535–1545 (WA 42:466.33–467.2)

Compare further
Genesis 4:26: LW 1:328–31; WA 42:241–43
Genesis 13:4: LW 2:332–34; WA 42, 499–501
Genesis 21:33–34: LW 4:90; WA 43:199–200

---

[44] The Vulgate has *et invocavit nomen eius*.

Abraham was effective as a missionary in Egypt

Genesis 12:14–16 (NIV): When Abram came to Egypt, the Egyptians saw that she was a very beautiful woman. And when Pharaoh's officials saw her, they praised her to Pharaoh, and she was taken into his palace. He treated Abram well for her sake, and Abram acquired sheep and cattle, male and female donkeys, menservants and maidservants, and camels.

God is thus accustomed to deal with those who are his in such a way that he does not let them remain too long in one place. He chases them back and forth not only for their sake, in order to prove their faith, but also so that they may be useful to other people. Abraham certainly could not remain silent, and he did not consider himself unfit to preach to the people of God's mercy. Therefore, God drove him through hunger into the land of Egypt so that he might also be of some use there and enlighten some with true knowledge of God, which he also did without doubt. It would be insufferable for someone to associate with people and not reveal what is useful for the salvation of their souls. Since he now says that he lived in Egypt, and it went well for him for Sarai's sake, he did not neglect to teach them. God acts in wonderful ways on earth; he sends apostle and preacher to people before they themselves perceive or in anyway think about it. Even those who are sent do not know themselves how they have arrived there.

Predigten über das 1. Buch Mose.
(Sermons on the First Book of Moses)
1523–1524 (1527)
WA 24:261.26–262.11

Jacob preaches to the Gentiles

Genesis 35:2 (NIV): So Jacob said to his household and to all who were with him, "Get rid of the foreign gods you have with you."

Moses, moreover, says that Jacob spoke to his household and all who were with him. Here he distinguishes between members of the household and outsiders. The members of the household were his wives, children, servants, and maids. By others "who were with him" he means those whose hearts God had touched so that they joined themselves to Jacob's house, either because of the hope of intermarriage or because they were added from the booty and spoils of the Shechemites. For I have often stated that it is quite credible that when the patriarchs were teaching, many of the heathen flocked to them, for they saw that the patriarchs were godly and holy men and that God was with them, and therefore they heard and embraced their doctrine.

For when ambassadors and preachers were sent by God into the world, we must not think that their ministry passed away without fruit. Not only were those joined to them who were of the blood of the patriarchs but also outsiders such as those who were confederates of Abraham above [chapter 14:13], Eshcol and Aner, who all undoubtedly heard the Word, and likewise Abimelech. Later on, Joseph in Egypt, Daniel in Babylon, and Jonah in Nineveh taught the doctrine of God. Therefore God gathered a church in the world not only from the one family of the patriarchs but from all nations to which the Word made its way.

Lectures on Genesis (LW 6:227)
Genesis-Vorlesung 1535–1545 (WA 44:168.14–29)

Mary and Joseph were missionaries in Egypt like the Wise Men were in their land. Persecution leads to the expansion of the church.

Moreover God wants to watch over his Word and church in spite of the tyrants' evilness, so that they still let the church and Word remain. Yes, even more, their onslaught and persecution give rise to the expansion of the church and the further dissemination of God's Word.

There is no doubt that Mary and Joseph and perhaps others with them that had come to know the child were not silent while in Egypt over the great miracle which had occurred with this child. They preached and brought others to faith and salvation, just as the Wise Men in particular were certainly preachers of the New Testament in their land and diligently taught their people about this child. Although he is determined to suppress it, this news gives reason for Herod to feign ignorance. The same still happens today. When the tyrants rage against the Gospel, they do no more than blow into the ashes whereby the fire grows and the ashes invade their eyes. This is what befalls their tyranny: When they spill innocent blood, this blood of Christians becomes like dung which fertilizes the field so that it is enriched and yields a good crop. Through persecution Christianity grows, but where peace and tranquility prevail, there Christians become lazy and idle.

Predigt am Tage der unschuldigen Kinder über Matthäus 2, 13–23
(Sermon on the Day of Holy Innocents)
Hauspostille (House Postil) 1544
WA 52:602.8–26

On the missionary effectiveness of the treasurer in Africa

Acts 8:39 (NIV): But [he] went on his way rejoicing.

If the eunuch that was converted by Philip remained a real Christian, which is exactly what one would assume, then he without a doubt taught many others God's Word since he was commanded "to proclaim the deeds of the one who calls us out of the darkness into his wonderful light" (1 Peter 2:9). The faith of many was surely a result of his preaching because the Word of God does not return empty (Isaiah 55:11). From faith, the church follows. The church, therefore, through the Word had the offices to baptize, to teach, and all the remaining offices mentioned above. She fulfilled them all. All of this the eunuch effected by means of no other authority than the authority of his baptism and of his faith, especially since none others were there who could have done this.

De instituendis ministris ecclesiae
(On the institution of the ministry of the church) 1523
WA 12:192.15–23

A Christian lives for the sake of proclamation

1 Peter 2:9: That you should proclaim the deeds of the one who called you from the darkness into his wonderful light.

We live on earth only so that we should be a help to other people. Otherwise, it would be best if God would strangle us and let us die as soon as we were baptized and had begun to believe. For this reason, however, he lets us live that we may bring other people also to faith as he has done for us . . .

This is part of being a priest, being God's messenger and having his command to proclaim his Word. You should preach the "good work," that is, the miraculous work that God has done as he brought you from darkness into light. This is the highest priestly office. Consequently, your preaching should be done so that one brother proclaims to the other the mighty deed of God: how through him you have been redeemed from sin, hell, death, and from all misery, and have been called to eternal life. You should also instruct people how they should come to that light. Everything then should be directed in such a way that you recognize what God has done for you and that you, thereafter, make it your highest priority to proclaim this publicly and call everyone to the light to which you are called. Where you see people that do not know this, you should instruct them and also teach them how you learned, that is, how one through the good work and might of God is saved and comes from darkness into light.

Predigten über den 1. Petrusbrief. 1. Bearbeitung
(Sermons on 1 Peter, first edition) 1523
WA 12:267.3–7, 318.25–319.6

Every Christian is bound by duty to give a missionary witness

For no one can deny that every Christian possesses the word of God and is taught and anointed by God to be priest, as Christ says, John 6 [:45], "They shall all be taught by God," and Psalm 45 [:7], "God has anointed you with the oil of gladness on account of your fellows." These fellows are the Christians, Christ's brethren, who with him are consecrated priests, as Peter says too, 1 Peter 2 [:9], "You are a royal priesthood so that you may declare the virtue of him who called you into his marvelous light."

But if it is true that they have God's word and are anointed by him, then it is their duty to confess, to teach, and to spread [his word], as Paul says, 2 Corinthians 4 [2 Cor. 4:13], "Since we have the same spirit of faith, so we speak," and the prophet says in Psalm 116 [:10], "I came to believe, therefore I speak." And in Psalm 51 [:13], he [God] says of all Christians, "I will teach the ungodly your ways, and sinners will return to you." Here again it is certain that a Christian not only has the right and power to teach God's word but has the duty to do so on pain of losing his soul and of God's disfavor.

If you say, "How can this be? If he is not called to do so he may indeed not preach, as you yourself have frequently taught," I answer that here you should put the Christian into two places. First, if he is in a place where there are no Christians he needs no other call than to be a Christian, called and anointed by God from within. Here it is his duty to preach and to teach the gospel to erring heathen or non-Christians, because of the duty of brotherly love, even though no man calls him to do so. This is what Stephen did, Acts 6:7, even though he had not been ordered into any office by the apostles. Yet he still preached and did great signs among the people. Again, Philip, the deacon and Stephen's comrade, Acts 8 [:5], did the same thing even though the office of preaching was not commanded to him either. Again, Apollos did so too, Acts 18 [:25]. In such a case a Christian looks with brotherly love at the need of the poor and perishing souls and does not wait until he is given a command or letter from a prince or bishop. For need breaks all laws and has none. Thus it is the duty of love to help if there is no one else who could or should help.

Second, if he is at a place where there are Christians who have the same power and right as he, he should not draw attention to himself. Instead, he should let himself be called and chosen to preach and to teach in the place of and by the command of the others. Indeed, a Christian has so much power that he may and even should make an appearance and teach among Christians—without a call from men—when he becomes aware that there is a lack of teachers, provided he does it in a decent and becoming manner. This was clearly described by St. Paul in 1 Corinthians 14 [:30], when he says, "If something is revealed to someone else sitting by, let the first be silent." Do you see what St. Paul does here? He tells the teacher to be silent and withdraw from the midst of the Christians; and he lets the listener appear, even without a call. All this is done because need knows no command.

> The Right and Power of a Christian Congregation
> or Community . . . 1523 (LW 39:309–10)
>
> Daß eine christliche Versammlung
> oder Gemeinde . . . 1523 (WA 11:411.31–413.6)

The missionary witness is linked to prayer

For once a Christian begins to know Christ as his Lord and Savior, through whom he is redeemed from death and brought into His dominion and inheritance, God completely permeates his heart.[51] Now he is eager to help everyone acquire the same benefits. For his greatest delight is in this treasure, the knowledge of Christ. Therefore he steps forth boldly, teaches and admonishes others, praises and confesses his treasure before everybody, prays and yearns that they, too, may obtain such mercy. There is a spirit of restlessness amid the greatest calm, that is, in God's grace and peace. A Christian cannot be still or idle. He constantly strives and struggles with all his might, as one who has no other object in life than to disseminate God's honor and glory among the people, that others may also receive such a spirit of grace and through this spirit also help him pray. For wherever the spirit of grace resides, there we can and dare, yes, must begin to pray.

> Dr. Martin Luther's Exposition of the Fourteenth
> and Fifteenth Chapters of the Gospel of St. John (LW 24:87–88)
>> Das 14. und 15. Kapitel S. Johannis gepredigt
>> und ausgelegt (1537) 1538 (WA 45:540.13–25)

---

[51] The German word is *durchgottet*; for an analogous idea, cf. *Luther the Expositor*, 185–86.

The Movement That Began with the Apostles Continues Until Judgment Day

As a stone that falls in the water

Mark 16:15 (NIV): Go into all the world and preach the good news to all creation.

Here arises a question about this saying, "Go into all the world." How is one to understand this question since the apostles have not actually reached the whole world? Moreover, many islands have been found in our time that are inhabited by heathen, but no one has preached to them, yet the Scripture nevertheless says that "Their word has gone out to the ends of the earth" (Romans 10:18).

Answer: Their preaching went out to the whole world even though it has not yet reached the whole world. This outcome has begun and its goal is set though it is not yet completed and accomplished; instead, it shall be extended through preaching even farther until the Day of Judgment. When this preaching reaches all corners of the world and is heard and pronounced, then it is complete and in every respect finished and the Last Day will also arrive.

With this message or preaching, it is just as if one throws a stone into the water. It makes waves and circles or wheels around itself, and the waves roll always farther outward. One drives the other until they reach the shore. Although it is still in the middle, the waves do not rest; instead, the waves continue forward. So it is with the preaching. It is started through the apostles and always proceeds and is driven farther through the preacher to and fro in the world, driven out and persecuted; nevertheless, it is always being made more widely known to those that have never heard it before. As it travels, however, in the center, it may be extinguished and perverted by heresy. Or as it is said, if someone sends a message out, the message has been sent even though it has not arrived at the intended place or at a particular point, but is traveling en route, as when one says: "The emperor's message has gone out," though it has not yet arrived at Nuremberg or in Turkey where it now should go. This is how the preaching of the apostles should also be understood.

Himmelfahrtspredigt (Ascension Sermon), May 29, 1522
Evangelienpostille (Postil on the Gospels)
WA 10/3:139.17–140.16

COMPARE FURTHER
Himmelfahrtspredigt, May 25, 1525: WA 17/1:257f.
Himmelfahrtspredigt, May 22, 1533: WA 37/1:77f.

The kingdom of Christ is a constant happening

John 10:16 (NIV): I have other sheep that are not of this sheep pen. I must bring them also.

He says that the Gospel should also be preached to the Gentiles, that they also should believe in Christ, so that there shall be *one* Christian congregation out of Jews and Gentiles. Afterward, he accomplished this through the apostles, who preached to the Gentiles and converted them to faith. Everything is therefore one church or congregation, one faith, one hope, one love, one baptism, and such things. This remains true today and always until Judgment Day. You must therefore not understand it in such a way that the whole world and all people will believe in Christ. Because we must always have the holy cross, the greater portion will always be those who persecute Christians. Consequently, one must always preach the Gospel so that one may bring some more to become Christians. The kingdom of Christ stands in becoming, not in being. This is a short explanation of the Gospel.

Sermon von dem guten Hirten
(Sermon on the Good Shepherd) 1523
WA 12:540.3–15

We are still calling today

Matthew 22:9 (NIV): Go to the street corners and invite to the banquet anyone you find.

It does not say here that we were also previously invited but that now the invitation is passing from the Jewish people to the Gentiles, where Scripture and the Law have not been. Paul says that it was not promised to us Gentiles; neither were we previously invited through Scripture. We have been invited, however, through the apostles, and they call to whomever they still find whether or not they are now guests. That is the Gospel which has been preached through the whole world. "Evil and Good," he says, "they gathered."

It is still not finished. This time period continues in which the servants go to the streets. The apostles began, and we call together to the present day. The tables will be full when the advent of the Last Day arrives and the Gospel is known in the whole world.

When that is finished, then the tables will be full, no more will be invited, and nothing will be missing. Then the words will have no more power, but that which follows will come to pass: "The king came in to inspect the guests." This will happen on the Last Day. The tables will be examined, but not yet. Now we see the preachers and the apostles, but then the apostles and the servants will not be evident. Instead, he himself will enter into the spiritual wedding celebration, and he will examine all. That is, he will come to the Judgment. When the preaching has come to an end, then he will see two kinds of people: One kind will be adorned with a wedding garment, the other not.

Predigt am Sonntag vor Simon und Judas
(Sermon on Sunday before Simon and Jude) October 22, 1525
WA 17/1:442.31–443.9

The Preaching of Christ is God's blessing for all people—as preaching of Law and Gospel

The whole of theology is therein summarized

Genesis 22:18 (NIV): And through your offspring all nations on earth will be blessed.

When God speaks, he opens his mouth wide. It is not of limited extent but applies to the whole world, which he includes totally in his curse. As Paul says, "Scripture has enclosed everything under sin in order that the promise might be given through faith in Jesus Christ" (Romans 11:32 and Galatians 3:22). He does not actually curse but shows us what we are, namely, that we are completely under the curse. He wants to bless, indeed, not just two or three peoples, but the entire world . . .

The blessing is now supposed to have been extended over all the Gentiles, indeed, in such a way that it occurs in Abraham's name. This is the Gospel. However, the verse does not imply that all heathen will accept the blessing. St. Paul is a master at interpreting such passages. "It is herein promised," he says (Romans 10:18), "that God wills that the Gospel should go out." He does not say: "Everyone will accept it." The Gospel is a special kind of word which offers God's grace and mercy merited through Jesus Christ and acquired through his blood. He is the Lamb of God that bears the world's sin. Furthermore, he makes it known to all the world: If you believe and trust in me to the exclusion of works, then you are blessed and freed from death and all misfortune. The blessing has gone the breadth of the world and has come upon the Gentiles as well as upon the Jews and still continues . . .

There are, indeed, few that accept the blessing. God greets all the world, but few thank him. Nevertheless, it remains true that they all are blessed. That is, it is brought and laid before all of them. On the other hand, the fact that not all have become Christian implies that they reject this special saving blessing and, for the most part, persecute it. It is not said, therefore, that God desires to convert everyone. St. Paul only declares of the Gospel that it is a cry, which he causes to go out over everyone. It is supposed to be pure blessing. Whomever it strikes, it strikes. He who apprehends it, has it . . .

You see, this is the Gospel through which everything, world and sins, death and devil with all their glory, piety, and good works, is laid low and condemned. It may be found that it comes not always as blessing. On the other hand, before and apart from all works, all the grace is established through Christ so that no one is to boast, but everyone is to thank God, who has supplied the seed through which the rich and eternal blessing comes. This is the whole of theology of which until now neither the learned nor the great schools have understood a word.

Predigt 1. Mose 22.
(Sermon on the First Book of Moses, chapter 22) 1527
WA 24:392.7–30, 393.10–17, 395.6–13

The preaching of repentance and forgiveness of sins addresses all people

Luke 24:46–47 (NIV): This is what is written: The Christ will suffer and rise from the dead on the third day, and repentance and forgiveness of sins will be preached in his name to all nations.

Such preaching of repentance, he says, should go out to all people. Here he truly reaches wide around himself and grabs hold of everything at once that is in this world, whether Jew, Gentile, or anyone else you wish. In short, no one at all is excluded. They are all together, as he finds and meets them—Christ excluded—under God's wrath. He says: "You are altogether condemned in your doing and being, no matter what you are or to what extent however great, however high, however holy you may be . . ."

Neither reason nor any lawyer would say that I am a sinner and under God's wrath and condemnation if I do not steal, rob, commit adultery, etc.; instead, he says I am a pious respectable man whom no one could blame and accuse of anything, even a godly monk. Who would want to believe that with such a fine, respectable life I deserve only God's anger if I am without faith, and that I engage in nothing other than detestable idolatry by such beautiful service to God and rigorous exercises that I have prescribed for myself by my own judgment without God's Word and thereby I condemn myself into a deeper hell than others who openly sin?

Therefore, it is also no surprise that when the world hears this sort of preaching of repentance accusing it, only a small part accepts it, while the great majority, especially the intelligent and the holy, despise it. They even set their heads against it and say, "Oh, how can that be true? Should I allow myself to be scolded as a sinner and a condemned person by people who came here with some unknown new teaching? What have I done? Haven't I in all honesty kept away from sin and occupied myself with doing good? Should that all come to nothing? Can it be that the whole world prior to us went wrong and that what they did and the way they lived were lost? Is it possible that God would drive the whole world into the ditch and say that they are all lost and condemned? Oh, the devil told you to preach that!" Thus they defend and harden themselves in their unrepentance and incur more of God's wrath by their blasphemy and persecution of his Word.

This judgment and this preaching nevertheless proceed and always press forward as Christ here commands. Wherever they go, they should simply preach among all peoples and direct everyone to repent, and say that no one is able to escape God's wrath or become holy who does not accept this teaching. For this purpose, he rose from the dead, to begin such a kingdom through which such things must be preached, received, and believed by those who are therein obligated and ordained to be holy, though the world, the devil or hell be angered thereby . . .

After this, the other portion should follow, namely, that Christ commands the forgiveness of sins to be preached. It is not enough only to speak of sins and God's wrath and to terrify people . . . It is not Christ the Lord's intention to preach repentance in a way so that one should cause the conscience to remain in terror, but that one once again comfort and stand upright those who now recognize their sin and have contrite hearts . . .

This is the comforting preaching of the Gospel, which a person cannot understand by himself, as he does the preaching of the Law when it strikes his heart because it has been implanted in his nature from the beginning. Much more, the Gospel is a special revelation and the genuine personal voice of Christ. Human nature and reason cannot raise themselves above the judgment of the Law that concludes here and says, "Whoever is a sinner is condemned by God and so all people would have to remain under eternal wrath and condemnation if it were not for a different and new preaching being given from heaven." Only God's Son himself could institute this preaching and command that it spread through the world. In it God offers grace and mercy to those who feel their sins and God's anger . . .

If God's wrath is taken from me, however, and I am to receive grace and forgiveness, then it must be paid off through someone. God cannot be gracious and merciful or remove the penalty and wrath unless it is paid for and satisfaction is made. Now no one could have made compensation for the eternal and irreparable damages and God's eternal wrath which we have made with our sins, not even an angel in heaven, but only the eternal person of God's Son himself, and indeed in such a way that he placed himself in our place, took our sins upon himself, and declared that he himself was responsible for them, etc. Our dear Lord and personal Savior and Mediator before God, Christ, did this with his blood and death. He became a sacrifice for us and through his purity, innocence, and righteousness, which was godly and eternal, canceled out all sins and wrath. For our sake he had to bear them, indeed drowning and swallowing and thus so highly meriting that God now is satisfied and says whomever he helps thereby, is helped . . .

Christ intends and herewith commands that such preaching should not be made known in a corner or to a special few alone, and not only to his Jews or few other nations. Instead, it should be preached in the whole wide world or, as he says, "among all nations" and again "to all creatures." He says this so that we know that he does not want to have anyone singled out or excluded from this who is willing to accept it and does not desire to exclude himself. Just as the preaching of repentance is a general preaching and is supposed to go over all people so that they all recognize themselves as sinners, in the same way the preaching of forgiveness should be universal and accepted by all, just as all people have need of it from the beginning up until the end of the world . . .

Finally, Christ also establishes here this preaching of repentance and forgiveness of sins for greater consolation in such a way that it should not be a type of preaching that is for only one time and is conveyed only once. It should, instead, always without stopping go on and continue in Christianity as long as the kingdom of Christ endures. Christ instituted it for this purpose and in this way so that it should be a continual, eternal treasure and eternal mercy, which is at all times effective and powerful . . . Christ instituted here such a kingdom on earth, which should be called an eternal kingdom of grace and always remain under the forgiveness of sins and thus mightily hover over those who believe here, that, though sins still remain in their flesh and blood and are so very deeply entrenched, they cannot be wiped out in this life, they shall still not bring harm. They are, instead, forgiven and not counted against us; admittedly, as long as we remain in the faith and daily work to suppress the remaining evil desire, until it finally is completely destroyed through Death, and this old bag of maggots rots in the grave, in order that the person may rise completely new and pure to eternal life.

Yes, if the person, who is now under grace and holy, falls again from repentance and faith and thereby looses forgiveness, nevertheless, the kingdom of grace stands fast and unmovable so that one can come to it again at any time, if one adheres to it through repentance and conversion. In the same way, the sun rises daily and not only drives away the night that's past but still continues and illumines the whole day, whether it comes in the darkness or is covered by thick clouds. Yes, even though someone locks his door and window to such a light, it still remains the same sun and breaks forth again so that one can always see it.

Predigt Lukas 24, 36–47
Crucigers Sommerpostille (Cruciger's Summer Postil)
(1544) 1531
WA 21:253.35–262.6

Reformation of Mission Practice

Matthew 23:15: Woe to you, teachers of the law and Pharisees, you hypocrites! You travel over land and sea to win a *single* convert, and when he becomes one, you make him twice as much a son of hell as you are.

Here the Lord also rebukes a vice. They thought that they had done a great and pleasing service to God in that they assimilated the Gentiles into themselves. It even appeared as if God's people were increased through this and as if they dissuaded many people from idolatry. Everyone would have to praise it, if one would bring the people from the Turkish faith to the Christian faith and would lead them from the devil to God, from sin to righteousness. That would truly be the highest of all and the most valuable work.

The Lord, however, does not let this lie. He says primarily that they move around through all countries to gain adherents to Judaism, and when they have done this, it is thereafter much worse for those concerned.

We therefore see here how the Jewish people have been dispersed and distributed very widely here and there and how they have converted many people in the cities among the Gentiles. This was their highest industry, as they brought many to their faith. They therefore traveled over land and water that they might make many adherents to Judaism. We should say concerning them that if the Gentiles had the Jews as neighbors, that they would have ruled by their Law. In the Acts of the Apostles one even sees that Jews were found in every community because they lived everywhere. There were from the Gentiles respectable people of both sexes, men and women, who took on the faith of the Jews. And from the Gentiles many people were turned to God that in the Scripture are not called Jews, but adherents to Judaism. They shared then in the Law of Moses and his worship of God. When it was the Passover or Pentecost or the Festival of Booths, not only the Jews, therefore, but also the adherents of

Judaism traveled to Jerusalem, and they brought a lot of money into the temple.

This has also happened under the pope, who out of all kingdoms wanted to establish the great, precious work that the Gentiles would be brought out of idolatry to the knowledge of the true God.

The Lord rebukes just such work here, though many of the Gentiles truly believed and St. Paul found the Gentiles tolerably prepared in the knowledge of Holy Scripture when he preached. Now it was no sin that the Jews preached the Ten Commandments to the Gentiles and taught them about the proper worship of God. It was, however, wrong for them to force the Gentiles to be circumcised and to keep the Law of Moses, as well as to have them bound to the city of Jerusalem. We have many examples in Holy Scripture which teach us the opposite . . .

One reads in the Acts of the Apostles that the treasurer of the queen Candace had traveled yearly to Jerusalem, though he was not circumcised. In the same way, when Naaman in Syria was converted by Elisha the Prophet, he did not compel him to be circumcised, but he still said, "From now on I will serve none, except the God alone, who dwells in Jerusalem." He, however, asked the prophet, "What should I do when I am in the temple of my king? Because I am his closest counsel, and so as he prays I must have his hand placed on my shoulders. Should I remain with him or not, since he worships the idol Nisroch?" Since he does not want to lay any law upon him, he allowed him to take to Syria with him enough earth as was necessary to make an altar. This was a reminder so that he would not forget the true God, who dwelled there in the land of Judah. Thus Naaman remained pious and godly in the midst of the pagans and discharged the duties of his calling and office. Purely by himself, he changed his pagan superstition and did it not only in the court of the king but also in the temple of Nisroch.

Jonah likewise journeyed to Nineveh. Daniel lived in Babylon, and Joseph ruled in Egypt, and did exactly this. They taught others the knowledge of the true God and that one should do away with idolatry. They, however, did not demand that the Gentiles observe anything except that they only believe in that God in which also Abraham had believed.

However, the Pharisees and the Sadducees commanded that the Gentiles must be circumcised, and they burdened them with their law. This is a fault for which the Lord scolds them since they force the people to do these things . . . The pope has done it in an entirely different way, for this is only child's play.

When the Gentiles here are saved through faith in Christ and believe that they must keep the Ten Commandments, they nevertheless assert that they must also have themselves circumcised, otherwise, they would not be saved. On the other hand, if now the Gentile had become an adherent to Judaism and did what he should have done, the Lord says, "You make out of him a son of hell, twice as much as you are." That is, he has become worse off afterward than he was before when he was a Gentile. This is what happened: Whenever it would come to pass that the Gentiles would come to the Jews and become adherents of Judaism and see their covetousness, usury, lewdness, and their other vices, they then would abandon the Jewish faith again and fall into such a horrible condition with arrogance, murder, lechery, greed, and their state would become much more shameful among the Jews. Among the Gentiles there was otherwise a much more stringent discipline and a more serious regimen than among the Jews. The Gentiles would become angry and say, "Oh, the true God is not here, as the Jews otherwise boasted." For this reason, they would fall away again from the faith.

Here the Lord says, "You do this with your greed, with your false doctrine and your arrogance. You consider the Gentiles your foot towel." Consequently, the Gentiles were again proud, and the Romans said, "Oh, we are nobles, who rule the land and people. What should this corner of the land of the Jews be? Only poor, miserable, and foolish people live there."

The Gentiles would have become fine holy people; however, because of the burden of the false doctrine as well as the vices and disgusting life of the Jews that was forced upon them, it became worse for the Gentiles. The high priest and the rulers were divided into two masses or gangs. One group, the Sadducees, did not believe that there was a devil, hell, or resurrection of the dead; moreover, they were the most prominent and the best in the church. The Pharisees, on the other hand, held the opposite belief. Consider for yourself, if a Gentile came among them and heard that they were disunited among one another and separated in doctrine, what would the Gentiles have thought? Likewise, if one had preached, "Bear in mind, one should live respectably in the world!" and they found such a shameful, disgusting condition with the Jews, then they would have thought, "Oh, they are knaves..." The sensible Gentiles would think, "I would rather remain with the teachings of Cicero and the philosophers. They even taught the immortality of the human soul. However, the high priests of the Jews deny it completely." Those who were and remained adherents to Judaism must have had strong legs. Nevertheless, the high priests boasted that they brought men to Judaism; however, it would have been better if they had never accepted that same faith before they were simple-minded, poor sinners, while they were pagans. When they fell away from Judaism again, they were doubly sinners, and the high priests themselves were sevenfold sinners.

Among the Gentiles, the public offices were so decently arranged that one would have been able to carry gold throughout the land on one's head. They therefore could surely also have traveled through the whole world and have brought many people to their faith. The Lord, however, says here, "If you did not want to make better adherents to Judaism, then you should not have bothered."

Thus it comes about all the time that the best of all works and divine services become the most abominable idolatry. What a dear, valuable treasure the Christian church has in the Holy Sacrament. It is the most precious jewel. Nevertheless, it has been made into nothing other than drudgery and plain perdition of the souls. It is the best of all works that the Gentiles were led out of idolatry to the knowledge of God. The Pharisees, however, did it in a perverse way. With one cast of the net, they took for themselves simultaneously the Gentiles' gold and silver, their money and goods, and then drove the Gentiles back again.

We behaved exactly the same way under the papacy. If we baptized people, then they were later misled through us. Since one had to believe in the articles of the Roman church . . . the Christians then thought, "The Christian faith was in any case difficult" because there are three persons in one Godhood, etc. The Jews also think, "Oh, it is much nicer under the Law of Moses than under the decrees of the pope," when they have heard these foolish things and articles that are against reason. We must, therefore, also howl against those who baptize Jews because they do not present the right, true doctrine to them. Besides this, they have seen that among us there is such an unfaithful life with thievery and usury that never would or could exist among the pagans.

In Cologne, a Jew was once baptized who through his riches came so high that he became the dean in the foundation there. When he died, he left the command in his testament to have a picture made on his grave of a cat and a mouse to indicate that just as little as these small animals would be in agreement, would a Jew remain a Christian.

One also reads of Emperor Frederick the First and of Emperor Sigismund, who had a Jew with him in his court. Since he now saw the Christian faith and it pleased him, he petitioned the emperor that he wanted to be baptized. The emperor, however, did not want to grant it to him for a long time. Finally, the emperor permitted it for him. When he had been baptized, the emperor had two fires kindled and said to the Jew, "Here are two fires, one for Christians and the other for Jews. Choose now into which you want to go. Nothing better can happen to you than after your baptism you go to heaven." When the Jew asked whether it could not be different, and the emperor said no, the Jew fell away from Christianity again and chose the Jewish fire. They see among us such scandal, disgrace, and depravity, which are much greater than the vices among them.

If a Turk would now come to us, then it would be difficult for him that he should hold the high articles of the Trinity, of the human nature of Christ, and of the sacraments. If now the mad, foolish doctrines of the pope are added to these, and he would see infidelity and such greed, then he would say, "I want to remain by my god." Who is responsible for this? You scared him off with our lying doctrine and our shameful life.

For this reason, we should be able to take the Jews at face value and also not forget for ourselves what shameful and improper doctrine and evil habits we have. Now they have been fine, reasonable people and not such asses as we.

One reads about a Jew who steadfastly remained in Christendom. This man was instructed in the Christian faith for more than a year. When the year had past, he said, "I must go to Rome and see the head of the church there." Then the pastor said to him, "By no means should you travel there because you might see something there yourself that would aggravate you and draw you away from Christianity." The Jew, however, journeyed to Rome. The pastor said, "Oh the effort and labor, which I have expended on him, are lost." After the Jew arrived in Rome and saw what an unchristian and evil life was there, he returned home again and said, "If your God were not the one, true God, then these people could not remain alive for a moment." He meant that God had to be gracious and merciful to be so patient and endure such things. This man bettered himself through this offense, and was baptized. He thought, "If God were not so gracious, merciful, patient, and forbearing with these sinners, then he would have destroyed them long ago, as usual all waters are engulfed by the sea."

There are many in Italy and in Germany that see how wickedly we live among one another and how one stabs at the other, and then they hear about the Christian faith, which is difficult enough by itself. Then they think, "Oh, what a holy and good doctrine there is here!" Since there are such stubborn people here, they are scared of it, so you hinder them with your shameful life and condition.

Thus the Jews behaved like the monks and nuns do in our time, who have talked the nobility and the rich into giving away their children so that they might have an even larger interest in the cloister. After they had then entered the cloister, they fell into such hate and envy on account of the life of the cloister that to this day one still has plenty to complain about this. They quickly regretted it. Furthermore, one does not find impatient and jealous people as well as idiosyncratic hotheads, such as exist in the capes and the cloisters. If one had left them outside, then they would have had to be humble, and a magistrate could have restrained them. For this reason only, wipe out the cloisters and make pious people in other ways, just as our doctrine says, if we would only accept it.

In this way, the Pharisees made pious people for the Jews, and they then became two times over rascals, just as now the pope has made the Jews doubly unchristian.

Predigt Matthäus 23, 15
(Sermon on Matthew 23:15) September 25, 1538
WA 47:463.7–468.3

II

PRACTICAL REALIZATION OF MISSION

The saving redemption is only found in faith in Jesus Christ, who through his substitutionary death on the cross has released us from God's wrath. Without this faith in Christ, a person is lost. While Luther emphasizes this exclusivity so strongly, he sees all forms that miss this faith in fundamentally the same way: as unbelief in the dominion of the devil.

Missionary opportunities present themselves, therefore, even in the immediate vicinity. A Christian must at anytime be prepared to lead other people to Christ. Every Divine Service is endowed with a missionary dimension. The whole life of a Christian in the ordinary way he conducts himself possesses a testimonial character because there are always people around that have still not recognized Christ. One can only take advantage of a missionary opportunity when one lives from the consolation of the Gospel and thereby masters the continual threats to one's personal faith. Every missionary initiative asks the question about the genuineness of one's own faith. Reformation and mission are bound together.

Two special missionary challenges presented themselves to Luther through his encounter with the numerous Jews in his own land and with the Turks in the great political and military confrontation. In both areas, Luther clearly insists on the preeminence of the missionary witness to Christ, and he himself employs it. In addition, he nevertheless advocates forceful measures of the worldly arm and with that causes confusion, if not also misunderstanding.

Congregational Work with Missionary Orientation

Missionary forms of liturgy

Now there are three kinds of divine service or mass. The first is the one in Latin which we published earlier under the title *Formula Missae*. It is not now my intention to abrogate or to change this service. It shall not be affected in the form which we have followed so far; but we shall continue to use it when or where we are pleased or prompted to do so. For in no wise would I want to discontinue the service in the Latin language, because the young are my chief concern. And if I could bring it to pass, and Greek and Hebrew were as familiar to us as the Latin and had as many fine melodies and songs, we would hold mass, sing, and read on successive Sundays in all four languages, German, Latin, Greek, and Hebrew. I do not at all agree with those who cling to one language and despise all others. I would rather train such youth and folk who could also be of service to Christ in foreign lands and be able to converse with the natives there, lest we become like the Waldenses in Bohemia, who have so ensconced their faith in their own language that they cannot speak plainly and clearly to anyone, unless he first learns their language. The Holy Spirit did not act like that in the beginning. He did not wait till all the world came to Jerusalem and studied Hebrew, but gave manifold tongues for the office of the ministry, so that the apostles could preach wherever they might go. I prefer to follow this example. It is also reasonable that the young should be trained in many languages; for who knows how God may use them in times to come? For this purpose our schools were founded.

The second is the *German Mass and Order of Service,* which should be arranged for the sake of the unlearned lay folk and with which we are now concerned. These two orders of service must be used publicly, in the churches, for all the people, among whom are many who do not believe and are not yet Christians. Most of them stand around and gape, hoping to see something new, just as if we were holding a service among the Turks or the heathen in a public square or out in a field. That is not yet a well-ordered and organized congregation, in which Christians could be ruled according to the gospel; on the contrary, the gospel must be publicly preached [to such people] to move them to believe and become Christians.

The third kind of service should be a truly evangelical order and should not be held in a public place for all sorts of people. But those who want to be Christians in earnest and who profess the gospel with hand and mouth should sign their names and meet alone in a house somewhere to pray, to read, to baptize, to receive the sacrament, and to do other Christian works. According to this order, those who do not lead Christian lives could be known, reproved, corrected, cast out, or excommunicated, according to the rule of Christ, Matthew 18 [:15–18]. Here one could also solicit benevolent gifts to be willingly given and distributed to the poor, according to St. Paul's example, 2 Corinthians 9. Here would be no need of much and elaborate singing. Here one could set up a brief and neat order for baptism and the sacrament and center everything on the Word, prayer, and love. Here one would need a good short catechism on the Creed, the Ten Commandments, and the Our Father.

In short, if one had the kind of people and persons who wanted to be Christians in earnest, the rules and regulations would soon be ready. But as yet I neither can nor desire to begin such a congregation or assembly or to make rules for it. For I have not yet the people or persons for it, nor do I see many who want it. But if I should be requested to do it and could not refuse with a good conscience, I should gladly do my part and help as best I can. In the meanwhile the two above-mentioned orders of service must suffice. And to train the young and to call and attract others to faith, I shall—besides preaching—help to further such public services for the people, until Christians who earnestly love the Word find each other and join together. For if I should try to make it up out of my own need, it might turn into a sect. For we

Germans are a rough, rude, and reckless people, with whom it is hard to do anything, except in cases of dire need.

German Mass (LW 53:62–64)
Deutsche Messe 1526 (WA 19:73.32–75.30)

Catechetical instruction as preparation for missionary witness

And finally, I strongly urge that the children be taught the catechism. Should they be taken captive in the invasion, they will at least take something of the Christian faith with them. Who knows what God might be able to accomplish through them. Joseph as a seventeen-year-old youth was sold into slavery into Egypt, but he had God's word and knew what be believed. And he converted all Egypt. The same is true of Daniel and his companions.

Admonition to Prayer against the Turks (LW 43:239)
Vermahnung zum Gebet wider den Türken 1541 (WA 51:621.5ff.)

The singing of Christian songs as Gospel witness

God has made our heart and spirit happy through his dear Son, whom he gave for our salvation from sin, death and the devil. Whoever honestly believes this, cannot leave it alone, but he must sing cheerfully and with joy and speak about it in order that others might listen and draw near. If, however, one does not want to sing and speak about it, it is a sign that he does not believe and is not in the new, cheerful testament but belongs under the old, rotten, unhappy testament. Therefore, the printers do very well when they diligently print good songs and make them pleasant for the people, with all kinds of ornamentation so that they are stimulated to this joy of the faith and gladly sing.

Vorrede zum Babst'schen Gesangbuch
(Preface to Babst's Hymnal) 1545
WA 35:477.6–15

Hymns

To his disciples spoke the Lord,
"Go out to ev'ry nation,
And bring to them the living Word
And this my invitation:
Let ev'ryone abandon sin
And come in true contrition
To be baptized and thereby win
Full pardon and remission
And heav'nly bliss inherit."

"To Jordan Came the Christ, Our Lord" (*Lutheran Worship* 223.5)
"Christ, unser Herr zum Jordan kam" 1541
Evangelisch-Lutherisches Kirchengesangbuch 146.5
WA 35:469.33–470.5

"What I on earth have done and taught,
Guide all your life and teaching;
So shall the kingdom's work be wrought
And honored in your preaching.
But watch lest foes with base alloy
The heav'nly treasure should destroy;
This final word I leave you."

"Dear Christians, One and All" (*Lutheran Worship* 353.10)
"Nun freut euch, lieben Christen gmein" 1523
Evangelisch-Lutherisches Kirchengesangbuch 239.10
WA 35:425.18–24

Christ we should praise aright,
Son of Mary, pure virgin maid,
As far as the sun brightly shines
To every corner of our world.

1524
WA 35:431.17–432.2

May God embrace us with his grace,
Pour blessings from his fountains,
And by the brightness of his face
Guide toward celestial mountains,
So that his saving acts we see
Wherein his love takes pleasure.
Let Jesus' healing power be
Revealed in richest measure,
Converting ev'ry nation.

All people living on his globe,
Praise God with exultation!
The world puts on a festive robe
And sings its jubilation
That your rule, Lord, is strong and true
And curbs sin's evil hour.
Your Word stands guard and will renew
Your people's health and power
To live, Lord, in your presence.

Our praises grow from living roots
When we thank God by action,
Improve the field, grow righteous fruits
Drawn by the Word's attraction.
Oh, bless us, Father and the Son
And Spirit, ever holy.
May people ev'rywhere be won
To love and praise you truly.
To this our heartfelt amen.

"May God Embrace Us with His Grace" (*Lutheran Worship* 288)
"Es wolle Gott uns gnädig sein" 1524
Evangelisch-Lutherisches Kirchengesangbuch 182
WA 35:418.4–419.9

It was God's love that sent you forth
As man's salvation,
Inviting to yourself the earth,
Ev'ry nation,

By your wholesome healing Word
Resounding round our planet

You are the health and saving light
Of lands in darkness;
You feed and lighten those in night
With your kindness.
All God's people find in you
Their treasure, joy and glory.

"In Peace and Joy I Now Depart" (*Lutheran Worship* 185.3–4)
"Lobgesang des Simeon" (Hymn of Simeon) 1524
Evangelisch-Lutherisches Kirchengesangbuch 310.3–4
WA 35:439.8–20

MISSION PRAYERS

Your kingdom come

Therefore we pray here in the first place that this may become effective with us, and that His name be so praised through the holy Word of God and a Christian life that both we who have accepted it may abide and daily grow therein, and that it my gain approbation and adherence among other people and proceed with power throughout the world, that many may find entrance into the Kingdom of Grace, be made partakers of redemption, being led thereto by the Holy Ghost, in order that thus we may all together remain forever in the one kingdom now begun.

For *the coming of God's Kingdom to us* occurs in two ways; first, here in time through the Word and faith; and secondly, in eternity forever through revelation. Now we pray for both these things, that it may come to those who are not yet in it, and, by daily increase, to us that have received the same, and hereafter in eternal life. All this is nothing else than saying: Dear Father, we pray, give us first Thy Word, that the Gospel be preached properly throughout the world; and secondly, that it be received in faith, and work and live in us, so that through the Word and the power of the Holy Ghost Thy kingdom may prevail among us, and the kingdom of the devil be put down, that he may have no right or power over us, until at last it shall be utterly destroyed, and sin, death, and hell shall be exterminated, that we may live forever in perfect righteousness and blessedness.

The Large Catechism, *Concordia Triglotta*, 711.52–712.54.
Großer Katechismus 1529
Bekenntnisschriften der Ev.-Luth. Kirche
(Göttinger Ausgabe) 673.39–674.29

Lord, convert

The second petition: "Thy kingdom come." Say: "O dear Lord, God and Father, thou seest how worldly wisdom and reason not only profane thy name and ascribe the honor due to thee to lies and to the devil, but how they also take the power, might, wealth and glory which thou hast given them on earth for ruling the world and thus serving thee, and use it in their own ambition to oppose thy kingdom. They are many and mighty; they plague and hinder the tiny flock of thy kingdom who are weak, despised, and few. They will not tolerate thy flock on earth and think that by plaguing them they render a great and godly service to thee. Dear Lord, God and Father, convert them and defend us. Convert those who are still to become children and members of thy kingdom so that they with us and we with them may serve thee in thy kingdom in true faith and unfeigned love and that from thy kingdom which has begun, we may enter into thy eternal kingdom. Defend us against those who will not turn away their might and power from the destruction of thy kingdom so that when they are cast down from their thrones and humbled, they will have to cease from their efforts. Amen."

A Simple Way to Prayer (LW 43:195)
Eine einfältige Weise zu beten 1535 (WA 38:360.29–361.5)

The Missionary Witness Toward the Jews

Biblical teaching and Christian life must come together

Therefore, I will cite from Scripture the reasons that move me to believe that Christ was a Jew born of a virgin, that I might perhaps also win some Jews to the Christian faith. Our fools, the popes, bishops, sophists, and monks—the crude asses' heads—have hitherto so treated the Jews that anyone who wished to be a good Christian would almost have had to become a Jew. If I had been a Jew and had seen such dolts and blockheads govern and teach the Christian faith, I would sooner have become a hog than a Christian.

They have dealt with the Jews as if they were dogs rather than human beings; they have done little else than deride them and seize their property. When they baptize them they show them nothing of Christian doctrine or life, but only subject them to popishness and monkery. When the Jews then see that Judaism has such strong support in Scripture, and that Christianity has become a mere babble without reliance on Scripture, how can they possibly compose themselves and become right good Christians? I have myself heard from pious baptized Jews that if they had not in our day heard the gospel they would have remained Jews under the cloak of Christianity for the rest of their days. For they acknowledge that they have never yet heard anything about Christ from those who baptized and taught them.

I hope that if one deals in a kindly way with the Jews and instructs them carefully from Holy Scripture, many of them will become genuine Christians and turn again to the faith of their fathers, the prophets and patriarchs. They will only be frightened further away from it if their Judaism is so utterly rejected that nothing is allowed to remain, and they are treated only with arrogance and scorn. If the apostles, who also were Jews, had dealt with us Gentiles as we Gentiles deal with the Jews, there would never have been a Christian among the Gentiles. Since they dealt with us Gentiles in such brotherly fashion, we in our turn ought to treat the Jews in a brotherly manner in order that we might convert some of them. For even we ourselves are not yet all very far along, not to speak of having arrived.

When we are inclined to boast of our position we should remember that we are but Gentiles, while the Jews are of the lineage of Christ. We are aliens and in-laws; they are blood relatives, cousins, and brothers of our Lord. Therefore, if one is to boast of flesh and blood, the Jews are actually nearer to Christ than we are, as St. Paul says in Romans 9 [:5]. God has also demonstrated this by his acts, for to no nation among the Gentiles has he granted so high an honor as he has to the Jews. For from among the Gentiles there have been raised up no patriarchs, no apostles, no prophets, indeed, very few genuine Christians either. And although the gospel has been proclaimed to all the world, yet He committed the Holy Scriptures, that is, the law and the prophets, to no nation except the Jews, as Paul says in Romans 3 [:2] and Psalm 147 [:19–20], "He declares his word to Jacob, his statutes and ordinances to Israel. He has not dealt thus with any other nation; nor revealed his ordinances to them." . . .

Therefore, I would request and advise that one deal gently with them and instruct them from Scripture; then some of them may come along. Instead of this we are trying only to drive them by force, slandering them, accusing them of having Christian blood if they don't stink, and I know not what other foolishness. So long as we thus treat them like dogs, how can we expect to work any good among them? Again, when we forbid them to labor and do business and have any human fellowship with us, thereby forcing them into usury, how is that supposed to do them any good?

If we really want to help them, we must be guided in our dealings with them not by papal law but by the law of Christian love. We must receive them cordially, and permit them to trade and work with us, that they may have occasion and opportunity to associate with us, hear our Christian teaching, and witness our Christian life. If some of them should prove stiff-necked, what of it? After all, we ourselves are not all good Christians either.

Here I will let the matter rest for the present, until I see what I have accomplished. God grant us all his mercy. Amen.

> That Jesus Christ Was a Born Jew (LW 45:200–201, 229)
> Daß Jesus Christus ein geborner Jude sei 1523
> WA 11:314.26–316.1, 336.22–36

Common hearing of the witness of the Bible

While we are on the subject, however, we wish not only to answer the futile liars who publicly malign me in these matters but we would also like to do a service to the Jews on the chance that we might bring some of them back to their own true faith, the one which their fathers held. To this end we will deal with them further, and suggest for the benefit of those who want to work with them a method and some passages from Scripture which they should employ in dealing with them. For many, even of the sophists, have also attempted this; but insofar as they have set about it in their own name, nothing has come of it. For they were trying to cast out the devil by means of the devil, and not by the finger of God [Luke 11:17–20].

In the first place, that the current belief of the Jews and their waiting upon the coming of the Messiah is erroneous is proved by the passage in Genesis 49 [:10–12] where the holy patriarch Jacob says: "The scepter shall not depart from Judah, nor a teacher from those at his feet, until the *Shiloh* comes; and to him shall be the gathering of the nations. He will bind his foal to the vine, and his ass to the choice vine. He will wash his garments with wine, and his mantle with the blood of grapes. His eyes are redder than wine, and his teeth whiter than milk." This passage is a divine promise, which cannot lie and must be fulfilled unless heaven and earth were first to pass away. So the Jews cannot deny that for nearly fifteen hundred years now, since the fall of Jerusalem, they have had no scepter, that is, neither kingdom nor king. Therefore, the *Shiloh*, or Messiah, must have come before this fifteen hundred year period, and before the destruction of Jerusalem.

If they try to say that the scepter was also taken away from Judah at the time of the Babylonian captivity, when the Jews were transported to Babylon and remained captive for seventy years, and yet the Messiah did not come at that time, the answer is that this is not true. For during the whole period of captivity the royal line continued in the person of King Jechoniah, thereafter Zerubbabel and other princes in turn until Herod became king. For "scepter" signifies not only a kingdom, but also a hegemony, as the Jews are well aware. Furthermore, they still always had prophets. So the kingdom or hegemony never did disappear, even though for a time it existed outside of its territorial boundaries. Also, never during the captivity were all the inhabitants driven out of the land, as has happened during these past fifteen hundred years when the Jews have had neither princes nor prophets.

It was for this reason that God provided them at that time with the prophets Jeremiah, Ezekiel, Haggai, and Zechariah, who proclaimed to them that they would again be freed from Babylon, in order that they would not think that this word of Jacob was false, or that the Messiah had come. But for these last fifteen hundred years they have had no prophet to proclaim that they should again be free. God would not have permitted this state of affairs to continue for such a long time, since he did not on that occasion permit it for such a short time. He thereby gives ample indication that this prophecy [Gen. 49:10–12] must have been fulfilled.

In addition, when Jacob says here that the scepter shall endure until the Messiah comes, it clearly follows that this scepter not only must not perish but also that it must become far more glorious than it ever was previously, before the Messiah's coming. For all the Jews know full well that the Messiah's kingdom will be the greatest and most glorious that has ever been on earth, as we read in Psalms 2, 72, and 89. For the promise is also made to David that his throne shall endure forever [Ps. 89:4, 29, 36–37]. Now the Jews will have to admit that today their scepter has now been nonexistent for fifteen hundred years, not to speak of its having become more glorious.

This prophecy can therefore be understood to refer to none other than Jesus Christ our Lord, who is of the tribe of Judah and of the royal lineage of David. He came when the scepter had fallen to Herod, the alien; He has been king these fifteen hundred years, and will remain king on into eternity. For his kingdom has spread to the ends of the earth, as the prophets foretold [Ps. 2:8; 72:8–11]; and the nations have been gathered to him, as Jacob says here [Gen. 49:10]. And there could not possibly be a greater king on earth, whose name would be exalted among more nations, than this Jesus Christ. . . .

The second passage is Daniel 9 :24–27 . . .

Now let someone tell me: Where will one find a prince, or Messiah, or king, with whom all this accords so perfectly, as with our Lord Jesus Christ? Scripture and history agree so perfectly with one another that the Jews have nothing they can say to the contrary. They certainly are painfully conscious of their destruction, which is immeasurably greater than any they have ever endured. They cannot point to any transgression so great that they would have merited such punishment (because they feel it is not a sin that they crucified Jesus, and that they committed greater sins before that but suffered less punishment). It would be unthinkable that God would leave them so long without prophets unless they were finished and all Scripture fulfilled.

But there are still more prophecies, as for example in Haggai 2 [:9], where God says of the rebuilt temple, "The splendor of this latter house shall be greater than that of the former," which is also very conclusive; and Zechariah 8 [:23], "In those clays ten men of all languages of the Gentiles shall take hold of the robe of a Jew, saying: We want to go with you; for we have heard that the Lord is with you," etc. There are many more, but it would take too long to discuss them all clearly and at length. For the present the two prophecies just cited are enough for a beginning.

If the Jews should take offense because we confess our Jesus to be a man, and yet true God, we will deal forcefully with that from Scripture in due time. But this is too harsh for a beginning. Let them first be suckled with milk, and begin by recognizing this man Jesus as the true Messiah; after that they may drink wine, and learn also that he is true God. For they have been led astray so long and so far that one must deal gently with them, as people who have been all too strongly indoctrinated to believe that God cannot be man.

>That Jesus Christ Was Born a Jew (LW 45:213–15, 221, 228–29)
>Daß Jesus Christus ein geborner Jude sei 1523
>WA 11:325.16–327.3, 331.23, 335.31–336.21

The missionary conversation must not demand too much of our Jewish partners

In this activity, one should therefore proceed as if a Jew would meet you who would not be embittered or callous, whom you wanted to bring to Christ. Although it is necessary to believe the article that Christ is God's Son, nevertheless, I would want to be silent concerning this at first, and manage and conform myself to him in such a way that he first develops a love for the Lord Christ, and would say that he was a person like any other sent by God and what a good deed God has done for mankind through him. Now, if I might bring that to his heart, that he might be enflamed and have love and desire for Christ, then I would also want to bring him further, so that he might believe that Christ is God. I would want to deal with him in this manner for his sake so that in a friendly manner I may bring him to believe in Christ. If, however, he were stubborn and unwilling to hear, then I would have to let him go.

Predigt Matthäus 4, 1ff.
(Sermon on Matthew 4:1ff.) February 14, 1524
WA 15:447.11–22

Luther reports on his conversations with Jews

Jeremiah 23:6 {NIV}: This is the name by which he will be called: The LORD Our Righteousness.

Now since Holy Scripture and the Jews themselves, as well as also the holy Fathers and all writers, agree the name (Jahwe-Lord) belongs only, strictly speaking, to the godly majesty and essence, we have here in Jeremiah a powerful, sturdy blow against the Jews and an excellent, great comfort for us Christians. Here this article of our faith is very forcefully founded, that Christ is a true, natural God. I have discussed this with Jews myself, even the most educated, who knew the Bible so well that it could not have a letter in it that they would not understand. I held out this passage, and they could bring out nothing against me. Finally, they gave this answer and said that they believe their Talmud, that is their interpretation. It says nothing about Christ, and they must follow the same exegesis. They, therefore, do not remain by the text but make excuses. If they would remain by this text alone, they would be overcome. This passage has too strong an ability to prove that this seed of David is a true and natural God. He is to be named with the name with which the true, rightful God is named.

Predigt Jeremia 23, 6–8
(Sermon on Jeremiah 23:6–8) November 25, 1526
WA 20:569.25–570.12

The meaning of the Reformation for the Jewish mission

Now since the golden light of the Gospel rises and shines, the hope is at hand that many of the Jews will be honestly and sincerely converted and drawn in earnestness to Christ, like you and some others have been, who are the remnant of the seed of Abraham, which is supposed to be saved through grace. For the one who has begun it will also lead it to completion and not allow his word to return to him empty. It therefore seemed good to me to send this little book to you for the strengthening and reinforcement of your faith in Christ, whom you recently learned to know from the Gospel and into whom you now finally also are baptized in the Spirit and are born from God. I also would wish that through your example and your work, Christ might also be made known among other Jews, who were predestined, are called, and shall come to their king David, in order that he might lead and save them, whom our priests and Pharisees in unbelievable madness reject even though they are ordained for this purpose, so that this judgment might come upon them. Conduct yourself well in the Lord and pray for me.

A Letter to Bernhard, a converted Jew 1523
A cover letter accompanying the conferral
of the Latin translation of the script
"That Jesus Christ Was Born a Jew" (WABr 3:102.37–48)

Instructions on the Baptism of a Jewish maiden

To the beloved brother Heinrich Genesius, true minister of the congregation of Ichtershausen, dear to God, grace and peace in Christ.

In regard to the Baptism of the Jewish maiden, my dear Heinrich, I am of the same opinion as you, that she be baptized completely covered with linen cloth just as in the way one uses the linen towels in our baths that are called bath towels. This would be what I wish, that as she stands in a big, wide tub full of water with a linen towel properly covering her, she should have water poured over her, or while sitting in the water with the same cloth clothing her, she should have her head immersed through a triple immersion. Yes, the tub should itself be hidden, by hanging curtains on all sides around it, in the way that one is also accustomed to hang the curtains for household baths.

I believe that for this reason, the custom has still come to us now out of the old church, that we normally also clothe the children, which are baptized naked even now without any shyness, with such a linen cloth, the so-called *Westenhemd* (the christening robe), because originally all Christians were normally baptized in such dress. For this reason, still today the Sunday after Easter is named White Sunday or the Sunday of the White Garments because those who were baptized wore this garment throughout the whole week after they were baptized. It should also not be assumed that the Jewish people were so poor that Christ himself was without such shame among his apostles that they would have baptized adults naked.

It is in addition to this that we also put the dead in such garments as a reminder of our baptism, with which we were baptized into Christ's death, so that the resurrection of the dead is attested just as much in death as it is also in Baptism, since Baptism is nothing other than a death to a future life.

Certainly, see to it that the maiden is not hypocritical concerning faith in Christ because this race is full of pretense and deceit. Not that I would doubt that the remnant of Abraham is still there, which belongs to Christ, but because until now the Jews have repeatedly mocked our faith. Admonish her, therefore, that she does not fatally deceive herself. Should she, however, be found upright, then I would wish her grace and steadfastness. You could then impart to her in my name my greeting in Christ and my dear bond. Conduct yourselves well in the Lord.

From my hermitage, July 9, 1530

Yours Martin Luther

WABr 5:452.1–28

Conversion or banishment

Next to others, you still also have in the country the Jews that cause great harm. Now we want to deal with them in a Christian manner and offer them the Christian faith, that they might willingly accept the Messiah, who indeed is their cousin born from their flesh and blood and the true seed of Abraham of whom they boast. I am, however, worried that the Jewish blood has now become diluted and wild. This you should seriously offer to them that they may be converted and allow themselves to be baptized, that one may see that it is important to them. If not, then we do not want to tolerate them. Christ tells us that we should be baptized and believe in him. If we cannot believe with the same strength, as we well should, God is nevertheless patient with us.

Now it has been the practice among the Jews that they daily only slander and profane our Lord Jesus Christ. Since they do this, and we know it, we should not tolerate them. If I should tolerate with me those who profane, slander, and curse my Lord, then I would participate in the sins of others; I have enough sin of my own. You, noblemen, should not tolerate them, but drive them away. When they, however, convert, leave their usury, and accept Christ, we gladly desire to accept them as our brothers... We still want to practice Christian love toward them and pray for them, that they are converted and accept the Lord, whom they should properly esteem in our presence... If the Jews desire to be converted to us and quit their slander and whatever else they have done toward us, then we would gladly want to forgive them; but when they do not, then we should not bear with them or tolerate them among us.

Eine Vermahnung wider die Juden
(An Admonition against the Jews) February 15, 1546
WA 51:195.9–196.17

The Missionary Witness toward the Turks

The missionary responsibility of the pastoral office

Why don't those who think the word "tend" applies only to them go to the Turks or at least to the Bohemians? ... or are there no souls in Turkey or Bohemia to tend? Or does he (the pope) believe that only those already tended are entrusted to him? Why then was Peter not satisfied with the sheep that had been tended by Christ but searched himself for any that he could tend and teach? Why, I say, do they lay claim to the tending yet do not do it?

Resolutio Luteriana super propositione XIII de potestate papae
(A Lutheran resolution on proposition 13
on the power of the pope) 1519
WA 2:225.4–12

How righteous Christians should confront the Turks

The pope curses those who supply Turks and Saracens with iron and wood so that one would think that he honestly desires to do good for Christendom. If he, however, were Christ's vicar, then he would get moving, go there, and preach the Gospel to the Turks, being committed to it with body and soul. That would be a Christian way to challenge the Turks and to increase and defend Christendom. What purpose does it then serve for one to restrain the Turks physically? What have the Turks done wrong? They seize land and rule it temporally. We have to suffer the same thing from the pope himself, who oppresses us in body and life, which the Turks do not do. Furthermore, the Turks allow everyone to remain in his own faith. The pope does not also do this but forces the whole world away from the Christian faith to his devilish lies so that with respect to life, property, and soul, the pope's rule is ten times worse than the Turks. Were Christ himself not supposed to overthrow the Antichrist according to Scripture, and one would ever desire to destroy the Turks, one would have to begin with the pope.

Bulla coenae domini
(The bull *coena domini*) 1522
WA 8:708.27–209.8

It is chiefly a spiritual confrontation

O how gladly Christ would receive me at the Last Judgment if, when summoned to the spiritual office to preach and care for souls, I had left it and busied myself with fighting and with the temporal sword! Why should Christ or his people have anything to do with the sword and going to war, and kill men's bodies, when he declared that he has come to save the world, not to kill people [John 3:17]? His work is to deal with the gospel and to redeem men from sin and death by his Spirit to help them from this world to everlasting life. According to John 6 [:15] he fled and would not let himself be made king; before Pilate he confessed, "My kingship is not of this world" [John 18:36]; and in the garden he bade Peter to put up his sword and said, "All who take the sword will perish by the sword" [Matt. 26:52].

I say this not because I would teach that worldly rulers ought not be Christians, or that a Christian cannot bear the sword and serve God in temporal government. Would to God they were all Christians, or that no one could be a prince unless he were a Christian! Things would be better than they now are, and the Turk would not be so powerful. But what I want to do is to keep a distinction between the callings and offices, so that everyone can see to what God has called him and fulfil the duties of his office faithfully and sincerely in the service of God. . . .

For although some praise the Turk's government because he allows everyone to believe what he will so long as he remains the temporal lord, yet this reputation is not true, for he does not allow Christians to come together in public, and no one can openly confess Christ or preach or teach against Mohammed. What kind of freedom of belief is it when no one is allowed to preach or confess Christ, and yet our salvation depends on that confession, as Paul says in Romans 10 [:9], "To confess with the lips saves," and Christ has strictly commanded us to confess and teach his gospel. . . .

I have wanted to tell all this to the first man, namely, Christian, so that he may know and see how much need there is for prayer, and how he must first smite the Turk's Allah, that is, his god the devil, and overcome his power and divinity; otherwise, I fear, the sword will accomplish little. Now this man is not to fight physically with the Turk, as the pope and his followers teach; nor is he to resist the Turk with the fist, but he is to recognize the Turk as God's rod and wrath which Christians must either suffer, if God visits their sins upon them, or fight against and drive away with repentance, tears, and prayer. Let whoever will despise this counsel despise it; I will watch to see what damage he will do the Turk.

> On War against the Turk 1529 (LW 46:165–66, 175, 184)
> Vom Kriege wider die Türken
> WA 30/1:111.29–112.17, 120.29–121.1, 129.6–16

The Qur'an is to be tested by the witness to Christ

That Christ is the Son of God, who for our sins has died, rose again, by whom we live, that we are righteous through faith in him and holy through the forgiveness of sins, etc.: These are the thunderbolts that disturb not only the Muslims, but also the gates of hell. Muhammad denies that Christ is the Son of God. He denies that he died for our sins. He denies that he rose from the dead in order to bring us to life. He denies that through faith in him sins are forgiven and we are justified. He denies that he will come as judge over the living and the dead, though he believes a resurrection of the dead and a day of judgment. He denies the Holy Spirit. He denies his gifts. Through these and similar articles, the conscience must be fortified against the ceremonies of the Muslims. Through these means the Qur'an must be refuted . . .

I will perhaps say more, if Muhammad himself will come to me with his Qur'an in his hand. I hope then that our Gospel, which shines in such great light, before the day of the judgment will also make an assault upon Muhammad, the detestable prophet himself. May our Lord Jesus Christ do this soon, to whom be the honor in eternity. Amen.

> Vorrede zu Libellus de ritu et moribus Turcorum
> (Preface to the book on the rites and customs of the Turks) 1530
> WA 30/2:207.37–208.18

Prisoners of war as missionaries

I must here be of encouragement and give a word of comfort to those Germans who already have been captured or may still be captured in Turkey. They must follow the example of the holy prophet Jeremiah, who also wrote a letter to Babylonia and encouraged its Jewish prisoners that they should be patient in captivity and remain firm in the faith until the time of their redemption, in order that they not be scandalized by the Babylonian faith and worship. It was so grand and had such wonderful splendor that very many apostatized toward it. Then, as I hear and read, Christians also greatly apostatize and accept the faith of the Turks or Muhammad willingly and without force for the sake of the great splendor that they have in their faith. Pay attention, therefore, my dear brother. Be warned and admonished, that you remain in the right Christian faith and neither deny nor forget your dear Lord and Savior Jesus Christ, who died for your sin.

Study now, while you still have room and place, the Ten Commandments, the Lord's Prayer, the Creed, and learn them well, especially the article in which we say, "And in Jesus Christ, his only-begotten Son, our Lord, who was conceived by the Holy Spirit, born of the virgin Mary, suffered under Pontius Pilate, crucified, died and buried, descended to Hell, on the third day again raised from the dead, ascended to Heaven, sitting on the Right of God, the almighty Father, from whence he shall come, to judge the living and the dead, etc." Because everything lies in this article. From this article, we are called Christians and are also called through the Gospel to the same, baptized and counted in Christendom and accepted, and receive through the same Holy Spirit the forgiveness of sins, in addition to the resurrection of the dead and eternal life. This article makes us into God's children and Christ's brothers so that we become like him eternally and coheirs.

Through this article, our faith is distinguished from all other beliefs on earth. The Jews don't have it, the Turks and Saracens also do not, furthermore a Papist or false Christian or any other unbeliever does not have it but only the orthodox Christian . . .

We now also want to comfort them, that they should be patient in their captivity and endure and bear all their misery willingly for God's sake. Now, therefore, take note that where God ordains that you are captured by the Turks, carried away, and sold, that you must live according to their will and be a servant. Consider that you should patiently and willingly accept such misery and service, which is sent by God. Suffer for God's sake, and in the truest way possible and in the most diligent way, serve your master to whom you are sold, independent of the fact that you are Christian and your master is a heathen or Turk, as if for this reason it would not be proper that you should be his servant. Moreover, in no case should you run away, as some do and think that they do right and well thereby. Some drown themselves or strangle themselves in some way. No, do not let it be so, dear brother! You must consider that you have lost your freedom and been placed in the state of serfdom out of which you cannot wriggle out without sin and disobedience. You rob and steal thereby from your master your body, which he bought or obtained in some other way, so that it henceforth is not yours but is instead his property, as an animal or other of his possessions . . .

With obstinacy and impatience, you do no more than aggravate your master, whose servant you have become, and thereby make his anger worse. In addition, you shame the teaching and name of Christ, as if Christians were such wicked, unfaithful, false people, who do not serve but escape and make away with themselves as do scoundrels and thieves. They become harder and more stubborn in their own faith through this. On the contrary, where you faithfully and diligently serve, you will adorn and praise the Gospel and the name of Christ so that your master and many others, as wicked as they might be, would have to say, "Well, surely now the Christians are a faithful, obedient, pious, humble, diligent people." You will, furthermore, thereby make the faith of the Turks a disgrace and perhaps convert many when they see that the Christians greatly surpass the Turks with humility, patience, industry, fidelity, and similar virtues. This is what St. Paul means, as he says (Titus 3:8) that the servants should in all things adorn or be an ornament to the doctrine of our Lord.

Eine Heerpredigt wider die Türken
(A Campaign Sermon against the Turks) 1529
WA 30/2:185.18–186.18, 192.22–193.5, 194.23–195.6

III

THE HISTORY OF MISSION

Luther looks at mission as a fundamental life expression of the church, not as some sort of special undertaking that needs to be specially organized. The history of the Christian church, which has existed since the promise to Adam and Eve and which will exist and work until Judgment Day, is identical with the history of the transmission of the message through missionary proclamation. When Christianity is seen as the original and most ancient religion, the other religions do not appear as neutral territory that has not been reached by the Christian message, but as paths that lead away or deviate from the true religion or that establish themselves in revolt against the Christian faith.

Luther sees the history of mission in opposition to a history of a diabolical counter mission, which in his time took shape especially in Islam and the papacy, insofar as they set themselves in the place of Christ through unbiblical doctrine. In this struggle between the two churches and mission, Luther trusts in the strength of the Word of God and the power of Christ. He, therefore, assumes that in all lands a Christian diaspora has remained, even if other religions now dominate in them. Despite all oppression and persecution, the gathering of the nation of God continues everywhere through the Gospel. Luther draws his perspective of the history of mission essentially from the interpretation of biblical promises. It is a theological point of view. Because it is founded to a much lesser extent on historical facts and empirical relationships, the actual dimensions of the needs of the missionary do not really come into view. In light of this, the strong confidence in the strength of the Word of God nevertheless must be tried and tested by a lively missionary practice.

The Mission Stretches Through All Time from the Beginning to the End of the World

From the beginning of the world, Christ has been preached and believed

We therefore can prove that our faith is not new and that we do not know of its beginning, but, on the contrary, it is the most ancient of all beliefs, which began at and has been preserved from the beginning of the world. When Adam and Eve, our first parents, came back again to grace in Paradise after their pitiful fall, they began this faith in the Savior, the Son of God. The promise that was given to them said, "The offspring of the woman shall trample the head of the serpent" (Genesis 3:15). From this first Gospel, our faith originated and flowed outward.

It is then made known and revealed from God himself that a woman should bear a son, which shall be called her, the woman's, offspring, so that the woman might, therefore, be a natural person and the child her natural son. Nevertheless, he is supposed to be the woman's offspring only, that is, not begotten from or through a man. He shall have strength and power so that he could and would trample the head of the serpent (the devil, who through Adam and Eve brought the whole human race into death and eternal damnation), which indicates his authority, and thereby redeem the human race from sin, God's wrath, and eternal death. That would certainly have to be a special individual and not someone simply greater than a normal human born from man and wife, but also greater than an angel because the devil, whose head he is supposed to trample, is himself the highest natural type of an angel . . .

This article concerning Christ has been preached from the beginning of the world until now and has been believed by all the holy patriarchs and prophets, namely, that Christ would be both true Man, as the woman's promised offspring, and also true God and Lord of all creatures, of sin, of the devil, and death. He was believed to be the one who was supposed to accomplish the reconciliation and redemption of the human race from the eternal wrath of God and condemnation that came over us because of the righteous judgment of God, and who should destroy the work of the devil . . .

This is, therefore, our sure foundation and comfort against all the gates of the devil and of hell, that we know that our faith in this Lord, whom we confess as true God and Man, is the correct, first, and most ancient faith and remains preserved at all times through the Son of God and is remaining as the last faith until the end of the world. The special godly power and work in it is plainly seen, in that even with such various daily and continuous persecution and opposition by the devil and the world, it nevertheless has prevailed and continues to do so. Even if from the beginning until now it has endured great, severe, and numerous storms and attacks, it has nevertheless not been overthrown by them or weakened but always continues and becomes stronger the more it is persecuted. It is evident that we, who are now at the end, praise God and believe exactly the same and even preach the same as Adam, Abel, Enoch, Noah, Abraham, and all the patriarchs and prophets have believed and preached.

Predigt Matthäus 8, 23–27
(Sermon on Matthew 8:23–27) January 31, 1546
WA 51:152.30–153.28, 155.16–28

The different religions must be derived from the one true religion

The origin of idol worship from true godliness: I believe that the worship of idols has arisen out of the highest piety. Where the fathers saw divine power in sun, stars, fire, and water, they praised God in them. Their children showed those creations respect, and their descendants, despite being ignorant of God, nevertheless, later worshiped the visible manifestations, sun, moon, fire, etc. with an external cult, until finally they worshiped onions and wild sows. Where the Gospel is not present, ignorance of God is so great in the human flesh.

Tischreden, Nachschriften von Anton Lauterbach
und Hieronymous Weller
(Table Talks as recorded by Anton Lauterbach
and Hieronymous Weller) 1537
WATr 3:417.22–28

Only the preaching of Christ actually makes God known

It is therefore not sufficient, and it is still not called the proper worship of God, how the Jews, Turks, and the whole world claim without the Word of God and faith in Christ that they worship the one God that created heaven and earth, etc. With that you have recognized neither his divine essence nor his will: That there is one God, by whom all things were created, you know from his works, that is, in you and all creatures. You may well see them, but you cannot externally recognize or experience him himself, who he is, what kind of divine essence he has, and how he is disposed.

If you know it and rightly recognize him, then you must hear his Word in which he has given himself to be recognized and says that he is the everlasting Father of our Lord Jesus Christ, whom he has given as intermediary, that he should be a true Man like us, though conceived and born of a virgin through the Holy Spirit without sin. Since in order for such a person to be truly an intermediary between God and humanity and our Savior that would redeem us from God's wrath and obtain for us eternal mercy, he would have to participate in both, that is God and Man, nature and essence. If, however, he has divine nature, then he must be almighty and eternal like the Father. In order that we might in this way recognize his divine essence, this mediator, God's Son, who is in the Father's bosom, has revealed it to us, etc.

Therefore, though Turks, Jews, and all heathen know to say as much as their reason can discern from God's works, that he is a creator of all things and that one should be obedient to him, etc. They constantly cry and slander us Christians, saying that we worship many gods—they treat us unfairly and unjustly thereby—we know, nevertheless, that they still do not have the right God. They do not want to listen to his Word, which he has revealed concerning himself from the beginning of the world until now through the holy patriarchs and the prophets and finally through Christ himself and his apostles. They do not recognize him in this way, but they blaspheme and rage against it.

They imagine a god, who has neither a Son nor a Holy Spirit in his divinity, and thus they claim that God is nothing more than a mere dream and worship it. Indeed, they claim lies and blasphemies as knowledge of God because they presume, without divine revelation, that is, without the Holy Spirit, to know God and to come to him without a mediator (which must be God's own Son). They are therefore fundamentally without God. There is truly no other God than the one who is the Father of our Lord Jesus Christ. Both reveal themselves to the church through the Holy Spirit and work and rule in the hearts of the faithful. As John (2 John 9) says, "Whoever does not continue and remain in the doctrine of Christ, does not have God." Christ says (John 5:23), "Whoever does not honor the Son, does not honor the Father," or (John 14:6), "No one comes to the Father except through me."

Such boasting of God by the Turks, Jews, and all unbelievers is therefore plainly nothing . . . since they deny Christ, who is true God and Man, and do not accept him. Thus they also have in God, whom they boast created heaven and earth, nothing more than a mere name or delusion of God . . . They do not want this God, who is a Father and gives his Son and has richly poured the Holy Spirit over us, but they slander and rage against him in the most horrible way.

The Jews also are most annoyed with us and cry that we have made three gods, since we worship the virgin's Son and the Holy Spirit next to one God. Nevertheless, they must know and confess that we have a clear witness out of their own Scripture, Moses and the prophets, and that we set these as the foundation of our faith so that Christ, God's Son, and the Spirit of God are called special, distinguishable persons of the divine essence, and thus their lies and slander are not against us but lie against and blaspheme God and the Holy Scriptures.

Predigt Matthäus 8, 23–27
(Sermon on Matthew 8:23–27) January 31, 1546
WA 51:150.38–152.29

The movement of the Gospel through the world before the coming of the end

Matthew 24:14: And this gospel of the kingdom will be preached in the whole world as a testimony to all nations, and then the end will come.

Before Judgment Day comes, the rule of the church and of the Christian faith must move over the whole world, just as the Lord Christ also said before in an earlier chapter that there will not be a city in which the Gospel should still be preached and that the Gospel shall move through the whole world in order that they all have a witness over their conscience, whether or not they believe.

The Gospel was in Egypt, then it was gone; furthermore, it has been in Greece, in Italy, in France, and in other lands. Now it is in the land of Germany; for who knows how long? The movement of the Gospel is now among us, but our ungratefulness and scorning of the divine Word, pettiness, and decadence make it so that it will not remain for long. There shall then follow after it a large rabble, and great wars will come later. In Africa, the Gospel was very powerfully present, but the liars corrupted it, and after it the Vandals and the wars came. It went likewise also in Egypt: first lying and then murder. It will also go exactly the same way in the German land. The pious preachers will first be taken away, and false prophets, enthusiasts, and demagogues will step into my place and that of other preachers and divide the church and tear it apart. Then there will also be added to it wars, so that princes will make war among themselves. Even the Turks will teach them manners before the movement in the world is finished. Then Judgment Day will come. St. Paul (Romans 11:25) also says that the Gospel must be preached through the whole world in order that all the Gentiles may experience it, so that the fullness of the Gentiles may also enter into heaven.

Christ is like the thresher. First, he beats out the ears with the flail. After that he also throws the chaff in a pile and gives it to the sows to eat. John the Baptist, the apostles, and all Christian preachers have done likewise. They are all threshers, for the Gospel gathers many to the kingdom of God, into the barn of the heavenly kingdom. When they have done this, then there is nothing left over, except chaff. Thereafter, marauding bands and sects will come and devour the chaff—the ungrateful and godless people. Do not doubt, God will have gathered his kernels already long before this.

Predigt Matthäus 24, 8ff.
(Sermon on Matthew 24:8ff.) 1539
WA 47:565.11–566.3

The end of the preaching of the Gospel is near

The condition of the Gospel at the present time is like that of a person that is ready to die. His soul rests on his lips, so that moving his lips only a little bit, he whispers the words, "Into your hands I commend my spirit, etc." Thus we are also the last movement of the Gospel, which confesses Christ. We call on Christ and praise him still a little longer. After this, the Last Day will soon follow.

Tischreden aus Johannes Aurifabers Sammlung
(Table Talks taken from Johann Aurifaber's collection)
WATr 6:135.1–7

I maintain that the Last Day is not far off because the Gospel is offering up its final strength, and it is like a candle. When it is about to burn out, it makes a great thrust at the last, just as if it were going to burn yet a long time, but in this way it dies. Thus it also appears with the Gospel, as if it would now extend itself widely. I am concerned, however, that it may die in the same way with a "whoosh" and thereby the Judgment Day shall come. It is the same way with a sick person. When he dies, he usually seems the freshest at the end, as if he would again recover, but in a "whoosh" he is gone.

Tischreden, Nachschriften von Kaspar Heydenreich
(Table Talks as recorded by Kaspar Heydenreich) 1542
WATr 5:184.4–12

The Church of God Must Resist the Church of Satan

Mission and reformation are closely connected. This is already demonstrated by the biblical example of Egypt.

> Genesis 41:45b (NIV): Pharaoh . . . gave [Joseph] Asenath daughter of Potiphera, priest of On, to be his wife.

Accordingly, although Asenath was a godless woman and not yet imbued with the pure knowledge of godliness, yet Joseph married her without sin and later taught her about the worship and invocation of the true God. Moreover, it is possible that many of the priests, when they heard Joseph teaching and admired so many excellent virtues in him, were converted to godliness from the worship of idols. Thus David says in Ps.105:22 that Joseph was a bishop of bishops and a teacher of teachers.

And the godliness of the king, or whatever light there was, can be discerned from his own words when he said above (v. 38) that Joseph had the Spirit of God. From this it is clear that he did not worship many gods, for his words are those of one who worships God purely. Perhaps some traces and remnants of the doctrine of the fathers handed down by Abraham remained in Egypt, even though some darkness crept in, as takes place in the propagation of religion when the devil continually mixes in tares. Today the purified doctrine of the Gospel has enlightened many who were oppressed by the tyranny of the Antichrist; but at the same time also there have gone out from us the Anabaptists, the Sacramentarians, and other fanatics, who have openly handed down godless teachings about the Trinity and the incarnation of Christ. They have not arisen from our midst. Yet for a time they were with us. But they have not sought purity of doctrine. No, they have sought their own glory and fame.

Thus the Egyptians first heard the pure doctrine and the promises from Abraham; but later these were obscured by false teachers, until at last there was a purification through Joseph.

Therefore I gather from this that Joseph was the husband of a saintly and godly woman, whether she was instructed by him before their marriage or later.

Lectures on Genesis (LW 7:200)
Genesis-Vorlesung (WA 44:447.18–39)

The church always lives in severe tribulation

After Adam and Eve from the beginning had taught and preached faith in the promised offspring to their children and children's children and to all people until the seventh patriarch Enoch, while through Cain and his followers the devil severely attacked the church and also assailed and struck the little ship with his winds and waves so that it was almost no more to be seen and was almost to the point that it should sink, he sent another preacher, Enoch, through whom together with Adam he preserved the doctrine among the others, his pious children and descendants, and restrained the devil. After this one, he sent Noah up until the flood when once again the church suffered dire need; nevertheless, it was preserved in these few people through this son of God and righted once again. After Noah and his children, Abraham was called to preserve the church of God, and followed subsequently all the prophets, kings as David and Hezekiah, up until the Lord Christ and his apostles, who all have preached this one faith against the raging and raving of the devil . . .

As was said, immediately from the beginning of the world, the waves of the evil spirit, who reigns in the air as Paul says (Ephesians 6:12), have struck this boat, which is called the Christian Church, to submerge it and to sink it with Christ and those who belong to him. It has at all times remained preserved against such storms in such horrors and such weakness as this, in which the Apostle Peter was, through faith and the call of this Savior Christ, the Son of God. One has had to fight against these winds and waves at all times. In all of these, the power of the Son of God has proved now for five thousand years that such winds and waves must one after another subside and cease.

So many have struck against it and have stormed and raged against it, which have now, praise God, at this time floundered, just as have the great, powerful empires and kingdoms of Babylon, Assyria, Greece, and Rome at the height of its power, but this boat nevertheless remained and still remains. That now the remaining storm winds of the Turks and the pope also still spew forth and spray their waves and have every intention of drowning this ship, we must consider this as the last raging and wrestling of the old Serpent, the devil, who has now almost worn himself out and run down on Christ and his church. He would gladly in his final anger and wrath do much evil; however, he knows that he must soon quit and must leave his poison and sting and bite in the feet of the Lord Christ and of his Christians.

Predigt Matthäus 3, 23–27
(Sermon on Matthew 3:23–27) January 31, 1546
WA 51:153.39–155.2

The last confrontation between church and antichurch

This situation serves well to instruct the conscience so that one is certain what the Turks are and what one is to regard them as with respect to Scripture. Scripture prophesies to us about two cruel tyrants who, before the Last Day, shall devastate and destroy Christendom. One is spiritual, with tricks or false worship and doctrine contrary to the real Christian faith and the Gospel. Daniel writes (11:36ff) of him that he shall raise himself above all gods and over all godly worship, etc., whom also St. Paul calls the Antichrist (2 Thessalonians 2:4). This is the pope with his papacy. We have, otherwise, written enough about him.

The second has the sword, physically and outwardly, in the most horrible way, of whom Daniel (7:7f) powerfully prophesies and Christ (Matthew 24:15) of a tribulation like which has never been on the earth. These are the Turks. Since the end of the world is at hand, the devil must attack Christendom most horribly with twice the power as formerly and give us the proper finale before we go to heaven.

Whoever desires to be a Christian in this time should fix his heart on Christ and think from now on not simply of peace and good days. The time for such tribulation and prophecy is here. Simultaneously also our defiance and comfort in the arrival of Christ and our redemption that is not far but will follow swiftly thereafter, as we will hear ...

Since the Gospel and the Sacrament, which is commanded by Christ, remains in a country, there are also certainly many Christians in that same country. As few of these as there may be, so will this country for the sake of their faith, preaching, and the Gospel, yes, even for Christ's sake whose name, Word, Spirit, and Sacrament are there, shall be called Christian and truly holy to God. There are also still in Turkey many Christians, more than there are otherwise in a country, as some are captive there and serve the Turks that have obtained them ...

The Scripture is in all its pronouncements fulfilled, just as at this time many signs have occurred, and such a great light of the Gospel is present in addition to such great blasphemy, willfulness, wickedness in the world as never has been and which cannot be worse. It must come to a crash and have an end.

Eine Heerpredigt wider den Türken
(A Campaign Sermon against the Turks) 1529
WA 30/2:161.31–162.19, 169.11–18, 172.13–17

THE WORLDWIDE GATHERING OF THE PEOPLE OF GOD

How Christianity spread through the world

Isaiah 60:4 (NIV): Lift up your eyes up and look about you: All assemble and come to you; your sons come from afar, and your daughters are carried on the arm.

Here he begins to list the lands in which the Gentiles have been converted to faith ...

This is now the meaning of Isaiah: "Look around yourself into the four directions of the world: So great and so wide I will make you, that you shall be in all the world. Your children shall be in every village." These words were said as encouragement for the first Christians at Jerusalem because they were despised and only a handful, in addition to being in the midst of their enemies, who should have indeed been their nearest friends, as follows in this chapter of Isaiah. That was a peculiar thing to behold, that the small group held fast to such a great, new thing and rebelled against the great multitude.

The Jews, then, having in mind that they would soon take counsel and stabilize the situation, began to kill them, to pursue and to persecute them in every place. They thought that it would easily happen that they could exterminate these poor, weak people. They did not see, the fools, that they thereby just blew on the fire that had been kindled and drove it into the whole world. With such raging and raving, they only gave fresh help so that this saying of Isaiah and God's will would be fulfilled against themselves. For by the persecution, the Christians were chased into the whole world, and the Gospel spread out so that in every locality the sons and daughters of Jerusalem were gathered to this light.

Isaiah 60:5 (NIV): Then you will look and be radiant, your heart will throb and swell with joy; the wealth on the seas will be brought to you, to you the riches of the nations will come.

Scripture has the custom that, though there are many and various seas, only the Mediterranean Sea is called a sea, without further designation. It names the Red Sea with a surname. The geographers have given the Mediterranean its name because it is in the middle of the earth. It separates the Evening (West), on the left side Spain, France, Italy, Greece, and Asia Minor to Cilicia; on the right side Africa and Egypt up to Palestine. On both sides it has very powerful countries and kingdoms, and the middle of it is full of islands like Crete, Rhodes, and Cypress. Presently the Turks have most of these in their possession. Scripture calls the Mediterranean "the sea." The Jewish land is placed toward Evening because Palestine is the end of the sea, and the Jewish nation adjoins Palestine toward Morning (in the East).

Now, these people on this sea, especially those on the left side, Scripture calls with the general name "Gentiles" because that which lives on the right side toward Morning has special names in Scripture. We are included among these Gentiles along with everything residing toward midnight to the left side of the sea. St. Paul (2 Timothy 1:11 and in other places), therefore, calls himself "a teacher and apostle of the Gentiles" because he preached throughout this same stretch on the left side of the sea and wrote all his epistles to there. He did not go to the other side, the right side of the sea (toward Africa). These are the Gentiles Isaiah means...

This saying of Isaiah is fulfilled for the most part through St. Paul. He is our apostle. Through his preaching, the multitude of the sea is converted and such strength of the Gentiles has come to faith. Everything is said as explanation: who the sons and daughters are, who shall come from far away, namely, the group of Gentile nations on the great Mediterranean Sea converted by Paul...

Before they were turned to the world; now they are clothed and turned toward the church...

Isaiah 60:6 (NIV): Herds of camels will cover your land, young camels of Midian and Ephah. And all from Sheba will come, bearing gold and incense and proclaiming the praise of the LORD.

Here he speaks of the peoples which come from the Morning because Midian, Ephah, Sheba, and the people that ride on camel beasts lie toward Morning from Jerusalem . . . In the way that the Latin and Greek geographers call all these peoples Arabs. They divide Arabia in three parts: *Arabiam desertam, Arabiam petream*, and *Arabiam felicem*; that is, desolate Arabia, rock Arabia, and rich Arabia. The desolate Arabia lies between Egypt and Judea toward Morning, through which the children of Israel were led by Moses, and only this is called Arabia in the Hebrew language. Rock Arabia adjoins Judea from morning and is a large country, but Isaiah is not speaking of either here.

The rich and largest Arabia, the one lying far from Judea on the other side of desolate Arabia and rock Arabia, is called in Hebrew "Sheba." Whether now it is so named by Abraham's or Ham's son is not important. Ephah is a piece of the same rich Arabia. Out of Arabia has come the Turk, Muhammad, and his grave was in the city of Mecca of the same land. It is named rich Arabia for this reason because it has precious gold and many valuable fruits, in particular, incense grows in no other place in the world other than this Sheba or Arabia. From here the queen of Sheba also brought many expensive spices to King Solomon (1 Kings 10:1ff). Now it is ruled by a Sultan, if he could assert himself before the Turks. Isaiah speaks here about this Arabia. The same people use camels and similar beasts. Midian, however, is their neighbor and borders with them on the Red Sea between Egypt and rich Arabia.

The meaning of Isaiah therefore is now that from these countries so many camels and dromedaries shall come that they will cover the land because of their great number, just as a large army covers the earth as it moves and encamps. Not that the camels and dromedaries come alone, but also the people that travel and ride upon them . . .

This bit we let be said of the spiritual coming: that the Christian Church will see, flow, marvel, and rejoice when not only the multitude of the sea from the Evening but also from the Morning the richest of all and largest people of Arabia will be gathered to her ... The meaning of Isaiah therefore must be that to the faith and the Gospel the people of this country of Arabia will be gathered with large crowds, and they shall offer themselves with all of their goods, camels, dromedaries, gold, incense, and whatever they have. Where real Christians are, they give themselves and everything that they have to serve Christ and those who are his. We see that also on this page it has come to pass that great possessions have been given to the church, and everyone gives himself and all that he has willingly and gladly to serve Christ and those that belong to him as St. Paul also writes of the Philippians and the Corinthians.

This epistle has understood the largest, most numerous, most powerful and richest people on earth as those the multitude that is on the sea and the strength of the Gentiles. That is approximately the core of the people on earth according to number and power. Arabia is thus respected as the richest and most noble people. With it, he indicates how the whole world should be converted to the faith.

Although the gold, incense, and camels may be understood physically, nevertheless, the coming and the bringing is to be understood as to the spiritual Jerusalem; however, we want to put the spiritual understanding in the Gospel. That he says "all from Sheba" does not mean that all have become believers, but that the whole land has become Christian, though there are those among them that do not believe; just as we say, "All Germany is now Christian because the old heathen ways are no longer in it." Although the minority are real Christians, it is nevertheless for their sakes called Christian. The Jewish people were also altogether God's people (Numbers 25), and there were indeed many among them that worship idols.

Finally, he says, "They will proclaim the praise of the Lord." This is the true proper Christian work, that we confess our sin and shame and preach only God's grace and work in us. No one can preach God's praise and honor who fails to recognize God's grace and this light. Nobody, however, can recognize God's grace who still retains something of his light, work, essence, and nature. That remains an old, blind, and dead Adam, who does not arise to see this light and preaches more of his own praise. Isaiah therefore praises here those from rich Arabia that are real Christians, who proclaim only God's praise, which without a doubt teaches this light of the grace and Gospel.

Predigt Jesaja 60, 1–6. Epiphanias
(Sermon on Isaiah 60:1–6, Epiphany)
Weihnachtspostille 1522 (Christmas Postil 1522)
WA 10/1.1:541.4–555.15

The gathering of a people of God from all peoples

[Zechariah 6:7:] When the steeds came out, they were impatient to get off and patrol the earth. And he said: Go, patrol the earth. So they patrolled the earth....

These, however, are the strong horses: Sts. Peter and Paul and John, the foremost and strongest apostles, who were sent into the Roman empire, where a great persecution of the Gospel took place. And for that reason, strong apostles were sent to this place; and St. Paul, the apostle of the Gentiles, was especially singled out for that purpose. Therefore, these men were given a special command to that end and were told, "Patrol the earth," that is, "the whole world." For at first the apostles themselves did not know that they were to proclaim the Gospel to the Gentiles, until they were admonished from heaven to do it....

[Zechariah 9:16:] On that day the Lord their God will save them, for they are the flock of His people.

This means that through the Gospel He will gather into one faith, as into one group or flock, those who have been scattered throughout the world and separated by various ways of teaching. For the Jews also were scattered about in all the world in their fashion and had various ways among themselves of getting pious, as one can see from the Pharisees, Sadducees, and scribes. But that is even more true of the Gentiles, who were separated throughout all the world into countless numbers of idolatrous sects. But when they were punished for that through the Gospel and their wrong beliefs together with all the cunning and wisdom of the old Adam was killed, then they were all brought together into an harmonious faith and teaching....

[Zechariah 10:9:] Though I scattered them among the nations, yet in far countries they shall remember Me.

The increase is to take place in this way: They will be scattered among the nations, like a seed which is increased in a field. This must of course be a spiritual increase, because they are not to return home from the nations but are to be sown there among the people and then increased. All of this takes place in this manner, that they will be sent by God among the nations as preachers and thus draw many people to themselves and through themselves to Christ. "For," He says, "they shall remember Me in far countries, that is, they shall preach and teach of Me, and thus they shall be increased and shall convert many others to Me." . . .

[Zechariah 12:6:] On that day I will make the princes of Judah like a blazing pot in the midst of wood, like a flaming torch among sheaves; and they shall devour to the right and to the left all the peoples round about.

Not only shall the persecutors rage in vain, but the Christians shall also, through the Word, harvest much fruit among all the Gentiles and shall convert and save many, and thus they shall devour round about them like a fire that is burning in the midst of dry wood or straw. The fire of the Holy Spirit, then, shall devour the Gentiles according to the flesh and prepare a place everywhere for the Gospel and the kingdom of Christ.

The Prophet Zechariah Expounded
LW 20:251–52, 296, 305–6, 326
Der prophet Sacharja ausgelegt. 1527
WA 23:583.7–15, 621.28–37, 629.17–25, 645.30–35

Now there are still many islands and lands that have been newly discovered

Titus 2:11 (NIV): For the grace of God that brings salvation has appeared to all men.

He says that it has appeared or been made known to all people because Christ (Mark 16:15) commanded that they should preach the Gospel in the whole world to all creatures. Paul also says in many places (especially Colossians 1:23), "The gospel that you heard and that has been proclaimed to every creatures under heaven." That is, it is publicly preached so that all creation would have been able to hear, so much more all people. Before, the Christ was only preached in the Jewish nation, and the Holy Scriptures were only with the Jews, as say the 76th Psalm (v. 2) and the 148th Psalm (v. 14). Afterward, however, it was set free and not restricted to a particular locality, but as the 19th Psalm (v. 5) says, "Their voice goes out into all the earth, their words to the ends of the world." This was said to the Apostles.

You might, however, say, "This did not actually happen at the time of the apostles. Was not Germany converted eight hundred years after the apostles, and have not islands and countries been recently found in which nothing of this grace has appeared in fifteen hundred years!" Answer: The apostle speaks of the nature of the Gospel. It is the type of preaching that was begun and so ordained that it should come into the whole world, and that already at the time of the apostles had arrived in the largest and best part of the world. Before this, however, no preaching of this kind had been started or ordained because the Law of Moses was composed only for the Jewish nation. Since most of this had happened and all of it would happen, as it then was happening, the Scripture describes it as if it had already happened. Scripture has a way of speaking that is usually called synecdoche, that is, when one speaks of a whole thing though it is true of only a part. For example, Christ was in the tomb three days and three nights when he actually lay there only one day, two nights, and two fractions of two days. Likewise, he says (Matthew 23:37) that

Jerusalem stones the prophets when, indeed, a majority of those in it were pious people. Likewise, he says that the clergy are greedy when there are certainly many pious ones among them. This is a common way to speak in almost every language, but especially in the Holy Scripture.

At that time the Gospel was preached to all creation because it was the kind of preaching that went out, had begun, and was ordained to come to all creation. In this manner, a prince might say that when an emissary is at his court and has gone out into the streets, "The emissary is off to one place or another even though he has not yet arrived there." Likewise, God has caused his Gospel to go out to all creatures, if it has not already actually happened yet. What the prophet really says is, "Their sound goes out into all lands." He does not say that it has already arrived in every land. Instead, it is on the way and goes out into all lands. Similarly, Paul means, "It shall be preached and be continuously visible before all people, and it is already on the way and has come to pass but just not completely."

Predigt Titus 2, 11–15
(Sermon on Titus 2:11–15)
Weihnachtspostille (Christmas Postil) 1522
WA 10/1.1:21.3–23.14

God fulfills his promise in the history of mission

Psalm 117:1 (NIV): Praise the LORD, all you nations.

This is the same as saying that God is not only the God of the Jews but the God of the heathen also, and not only of a small part of heathendom but of all heathen throughout the world. For to speak of "all heathen" is to exclude none. Thus we heathen are assured that we, too, belong to God and in heaven, and that we shall not be damned, even though we are not of Abraham's flesh and blood, as the Jews boast. As though only they, because of their physical descent from Abraham and the holy patriarchs, kings, and prophets, were God's children and heirs of heaven! To be sure, this distinction is theirs alone, of all men, that they are the children of such holy fathers. But the distinction of being God's children and heirs of His kingdom of heaven is not theirs alone. This psalm sings and proclaims that we heathen also have the very same distinction.

Now if all heathen are to praise God, this assumes that He has become their God. If He is to be their God, then they must know Him, believe in Him, and give up all idolatry. One cannot praise God with an idolatrous mouth or an unbelieving heart. And if they are to believe, they must first hear His Word and thereby receive the Holy Spirit, who through faith purifies and enlightens their hearts. One cannot come to faith or lay hold on the Holy Spirit without hearing the Word first, as St. Paul has said (Rom. 10:14); "How are they to believe in Him of whom they have never heard?" and (Gal. 3:2); "You have received the Spirit through the proclamation of faith." If they are to hear His Word, then preachers must be sent to proclaim God's Word to them; for not all the heathen can come to Jerusalem or make a living among the small company of the Jews. Therefore the psalmist does not say: "Come to Jerusalem, all heathen!" He lets them stay where they are and calls upon them, wherever they may be, to praise God. . . .

Thus we are faced with the fact that God sent His apostles and disciples to all heathen, had the Gospel preached, gave His Holy

Spirit, redeemed them from sin, death, and the devil, purified their hearts through faith, and thus accepted them as children and heirs and as His own people. He did not summon them to Jerusalem or command them to become Jews. . . .

Now see what a commotion this little psalm causes throughout the world—how it storms and rages among idols! The world has always been full of idolatry, factions, and error, so that even the Romans, the cleverest and mightiest of all, had more than a hundred gods. The world is divided into countless errors, and yet this psalm dares include these thoughts and boldly declare that all such factions and idolatries must cease, and that all the heathen must turn to one faith and praise and honor one God. Through the Word of God there is to come out of such a variety of worship one harmonious flock under one Shepherd (John 10:16). . . .

From this we see that the Word of God must be an almighty power of God (Rom. 1:16). It has cleaned up the idolatry, sectarianism, and error that then prevailed in the world so thoroughly that not a shred remains . . . . This is the greatest work God has done on earth, much greater than leading the Children of Israel out of Egypt, when only King Pharaoh and his followers were drowned in the Red Sea. But now the whole angry, perverse world has been drowned, and God's Word and Christendom survive. Let us praise such a work, and let us comfort ourselves with the conviction given us by this example, that God's Word will and must remain even though the devil and the world storm and rage against it ever so violently. The Word has done many wonders in the world, and it is not finished yet. . . .

Now how can it be true that all the heathen will become subject to one Christ and praise God, when all heathen persecute Christ, as He Himself says in Matt. 5:11: "Men shall revile you for My sake"? The answer: The psalm does not say that all men, or even all those among the heathen, will praise Him, but "all you heathen." That is to say: Wherever there are heathen—or a country or a city—there the Gospel will penetrate and will convert some to the kingdom of Christ. Regardless of whether all people believe it, still Christ rules wherever there are people: He preserves His Word, His Baptism and Sacrament, despite all devils and men. For the Gospel and Baptism must come to the whole world, as they have indeed come and every day come again. Thus He has said (Mark 16:15): "Go into all the world, and preach the Gospel to the whole creation"; and (Ps. 19:1): "The heavens are telling the glory of God, and the firmament proclaims His handiwork." That is, Christ is preached as far as the heavens and the firmament extend. Wherever one finds the Gospel, Baptism, and the Sacrament, there is His church, and in that place there are certainly living saints. There men praise Him, and He rules over them, even though they are but young people and children. Inevitably, however, there will be old people too.

You may say: "This is a small kingdom, to have so few Christians among the heathen!" Friend, this is not a small kingdom, nor is it an insignificant power. First of all, even for those few Christ must be in command, in order to have the devil, the world, death, life, and everything in His hand. Were this not true, the devil would not allow Christ's Gospel or His Baptism to last for an hour, not even for a moment; and the world would not let a single Christian live even for an hour. The persistence of the Gospel, Baptism, and Christians demonstrates Christ's almighty power over all devils and men among all heathen in all places, as Ps. 110:2 says: "Rule in the midst of Thy foes!"

A Commentary on Psalm 117
LW 14:8–11, 12–13
Der 117. Psalm ausgelegt. 1530
WA 31/1:228.20–230.33, 232.20–233.8

Epilogue

Already in 1625, the Wittenberg theologian Balthasar Meisner bemoaned the lack in Lutheranism of missions among Jews, Turks, and heathen. The situation has not changed substantially in the interim. Still today, the churches of the countries in which the Reformation originated make up the major part of Lutheranism. Emigrant churches in North and South America and Australia add to those. The actual missionary increase and the portion in the younger churches is very small in comparison to that of other confessional families. A completely different picture, for example, is offered by the Moravians that have relocated their numerical center outside the European sphere closer toward Africa and Central America. Lutheranism had extreme difficulty with its participation in the great missionary movement of the modern age.

This is not the fault of Luther's theology. His Reformation proclamation is in its inception so mission oriented that they would have immediately had the need to demonstrate its meaning for all people practically through missions. Several reasons may be identified why this did not happen: the expectation of the nearness of the Last Day, the ecumenical approach to missions that excluded special confessional enterprises, the shortage of personnel in the first generations, and then the incorporation into the state church and the failing of colonies of the Lutheran states. These, however, are not sufficient to explain the widespread complacency among the Lutherans. The impression remains that the missionary dynamic of Luther's theology was not able to carry itself through.

While Luther expounded the revelation of Christ according to its absolute uniqueness as the only message from God himself, which alone makes possible the salvation and redemption of mankind through faith in God's own saving work, he realized that the proclamation of the Gospel was unconditionally necessary for all people without exception. The simple chain of thought: "If He is to be their God, then they must know Him and believe in Him; if they are to believe, then they must first hear His Word; then preachers must be sent who will proclaim God's Word to them" (p. 100) incites undeniably a mission activity. With the Reformation's doctrine of justification, the church is at the same time made aware of its missionary mandate. It is no coincidence that the Lutheran renewal in the previous century called forth new missionary endeavors everywhere. A comprehensive knowledge of the world must awaken activities that remained unresolved in Luther's limited worldview.

The strength of Luther's view of mission is its alignment with Scripture and his unencumbered compliance with the biblical perception. A more realistic orientation with his own contemporary world conditions creates the possibility of perceiving the challenges more comprehensively. It, however, also threatens to make the biblical connection more relative. The concentration on one's particular historical situation together with the intention to promote one's personal interests will lead to the discovery of a new identity. Thereby, the universal solidarity of mankind before God is easily lost, and the consciousness of the commission, to proclaim the "alien" message of God to all as the only salvation, fades. The pursuit for our personal concerns even in the life of the church hides our missionary responsibility. The mission can only renew itself by taking seriously the power of the Word of God, which suppresses human goals.

Luther's repeatedly renewed reference to the necessity that a missionary witness must be credible is significant. Doctrine and life must agree. From the godless division of mankind, the Christian faith should bring us to unity. Luther warns against misleading the Jews and pagans through a "conversion" to Christianity to a more disorderly life and greater separations by means of bad Christian example. Mission can only be effective when it is accompanied by a continual renewal of the church and of the Christian. Mission cannot occur in isolation through individual missionaries without consideration for the church of the hinterland. The missionary witness is a common witness of Christendom. That which occurs in the established church may not be separated from that which happens outside in the missionary encounter with a non-Christian world. Moreover, the churchly internal world and the missionary external contact permeate each other in the modern, plural society. Thus the relationship between reforming, purifying revival and fruitful missionary activity will be seen anew.

Luther's view of religions, with his sharp separation between a natural knowledge of God obtained from the works of creation and the revelation of God alone in Christ and with the radical irreconcilability between the work of God in his Word and the work of the devil, does not appear to leave any room for a conversation between the religions. It places faith in hard opposition to unbelief. It, however, is exactly this conviction that opens then a solidarity between Christian, Jew, Muslim, and heathen. Unbelief always remains an acute threat and temptation also for the Christian, who is likewise attacked by the devil. Faith always remains under attack. There is thus a situation common to all, from which they may be led out only through hearing the Word of God. Luther's missionary method is therefore an invitation to a joint consideration of the witness of Holy Scripture for all who share this common bewilderment. Thereby, Luther is prepared to acknowledge that the non-Christian leads a more morally mature life—with respect to the commands of God written upon all men's hearts—than his Christian partner in the conversation. Luther then is also ready to make allowances for the previous history of his opposing partner and not demand that he accept all of the Christian body of doctrine immediately. Luther remains a realist. He knows that the missionary expansion does not continue undisturbed but must confront a defensive front and a countermovement. Mission is bound to the cross. He does not sketch a dream of a Christian world but helps to spiritually process the setbacks, disappointments, and repression. Luther does not hope for a world-improving societal reform through Christian influence because along with the positive efforts, he must also put up with the destructive force of the opposition. This soberness is more understandable today. Because it teaches trust in the Word of God against all appearances, it does not lead to a pessimistic resignation. Much more it exhorts the Christian unswervingly to emulate the example of Christ in living love.

Luther did not yet know the difficulty of a confessional and denominational mission. "Wherever one finds the Gospel, Baptism and the Sacrament, there is His church" (p. 102). This saying is still valid in ecumenical breadth because it focuses the view on Christ, who is effective with his power through the Word, and not upon the theological reception in the individual church administrations. Luther can only understand mission as the gathering of the one flock to one faith and to an appropriate living community in brotherly love over all human borders. "If one is not ready for that, how would one want to give a missionary witness?" he asks regarding the lack of social inclusion of the Jews.

Reformation and mission are not strangers to each other. They are conditioned upon each other, and in both cases it enters deeply into the same thing: The saving message of Christ is given to otherwise lost, sinful people. Just as reformation is always service to the whole church, so also mission is always service to all humanity. Luther desires to make this universal view clear. The Gospel does not belong in a corner, and Christ is Lord of everything.

The last verse of his chorale "Dear Christians, One and All Rejoice" brings this fusion of mission and reformation to expression with poetic precision, when it finally, with the view on the mission, says, "so that the kingdom of God is increased" and immediately appends the Reformation's warning, "But watch lest foes with base alloy, the heav'nly treasure should destroy."

BIBLICAL REFERENCES

GENESIS
3:15:   77
12:8:   15
12:14–16:   16
14:13:   17
22:18:   28
35:2:   17
41:38:   85
41:45:   85
49:10–12:   56–58

NUMBERS
chapter 25: 94

1 KINGS
chapter 10: 93

2 KINGS
chapter 5:   35

PSALMS
2:           57, 58
19:1:   102
19:5:   98
31:6:   84
45:7:   21
51:13:   21
72:          57, 58
76:2:   98
89:          57
105:22:   85
110:2:   102
116:10:   21
117:1:   100
147:19–20:   54
148:14:   98

ISAIAH
55:11:   19
60:4–6:   91–93

JEREMIAH
23:6:   61
chapter 29: 71

Daniel
7:7ff.:	89
9:24–27:	58
11:36ff.:	89

Haggai
2:9:	58

Zechariah
6:7:	96
8:23:	58
9:16:	96
10:9:	96–97
12:6:	97

Matthew
5:11:	101
6:10:	51
8:23–27	78, 81, 87f.
18:15–18:	44
22:9–11:	27
23:15:	34
23:37:	99
24:8–14:	82f.
24:9:	102
24:14:	82
24:15:	89
26:19:	40
26:52:	68

Mark
16:15:	24, 32, 98, 102
16:16:	48

Luke
2:31–32:	48
11:17–20:	56
24:46–47:	30

John
1:29:	28
3:17:	68
5:23:	81
6:15:	68
6:45:	21
10:16:	26, 101
14:6:	81
18:36:	68

Acts
6:7:	21
8:5:	21
8:26–40:	35
8:39:	19
18:25–26:	21
20:28:	28

Romans
1:16:	101
3:2:	54
3:22:	70
9:5:	54
10:9:	68
10:14:	100
10:18:	24, 28
11:25:	82
11:32:	28

1 Corinthians
13:13:	26
14:30:	22
15:3:	70

2 Corinthians
4:13:	21
9:6–9:	44

GALATIANS
3:2: 100
3:22: 28

EPHESIANS
3:8–10: 80
4:5: 26
6:12: 87

COLOSSIANS
1:23: 98

2 THESSALONIANS
2:4: 89

2 TIMOTHY
1:11: 92

TITUS
2:11: 98
3:8: 73

1 PETER
2:9: 19–21

2 JOHN
verse 9: 81

Selected Bibliography

Bienert, Walter. *Martin Luther und die Juden.* Frankfurt am Main: Evangelisches Verlagswerk, 1982.

Elert, Werner. *The Structure of Lutheranism.* Volume I. Translated by Walter A. Hansen. St. Louis: Concordia, 1962. Pp. 385–402.

Forsberg, Juhani. "Abraham als Paradigma der Mission in der Theologie Luthers." Pages 113–20 in *Lutherische Beiträge zur Missio Dei.* Veröffentlichungen der Luther-Akademie Ratzeburg 3. Erlangen: Martin Luther Verlag, 1982.

Holl, Karl. "Luther und die Mission." Pages 234–43 in *Der Westen.* Vol. 3 of *Gesammelte Aufsätze zur Kirchengeschichte.* Tübingen: J. C. B. Mohr, 1928. Also published in *Neue allgemeine Missionszeitschrift* I (1924): 36–49.

Holsten, Walter. "Reformation und Mission." *Archiv für Reformationsgeschichte* 44 (1953): 1–32.

Maurer, Wilhelm. "Reformation und Mission." *Lutherisches Missionsjahrbuch* (1963): 20–41.

Öberg, Ingemar. *Luther and World Mission.* Translated by Dean Apel. St. Louis: Concordia, forthcoming.

Öberg, Ingemar. "Mission und Heilsgeschichte bei Luther und in den Bekenntnisschriften." Pages 25–42 in *Lutherische Beiträge zur Missio Dei.* Veröffentlichungen der Luther-Akademie Ratzeburg 3. Erlangen: Martin Luther Verlag, 1982.

Wetter, Paul. *Der Missionsgedanke bei Martin Luther.* Bonn: Verlag für Kultur und Wissenschaft, 1999.